THIS SEASON OF
ANGELS

THIS SEASON OF ANGELS

Angelic Assignments During
This Prophetic Season

PERRY STONE

FaithWords

NEW YORK   NASHVILLE

FaithWords
Hachette Book Group
1290 Avenue of the Americas, New York, NY 10104
faithwords.com
twitter.com/faithwords
First Edition: October 2018

FaithWords is a division of Hachette Book Group, Inc. The FaithWords name and logo are trademarks of Hachette Book Group, Inc.

Unless otherwise noted, Scripture quotations are taken from the King James Version of the Holy Bible.

Scripture quotations marked (NKJV) are taken from *The New King James Version*®. Copyright © 1982 by Thomas Nelson. Used by permission. All rights reserved.

Scripture quotations marked (AMP) are taken from *The Amplified Bible*. Copyright © 1954, 1958, 1962, 1964, 1965, 1987 by The Lockman Foundation. Used by permission of Zondervan. The "Amplified" trademark is registered in the United States Patent and Trademark Office by The Lockman Foundation. Use of this trademark requires the permission of The Lockman Foundation.

The publisher is not responsible for websites (or their content) that are not owned by the publisher.

The Hachette Speakers Bureau provides a wide range of authors for speaking events. To find out more, go to www.hachettespeakersbureau.com or call (866) 376-6591.

Library of Congress Cataloging-in-Publication Data has been applied for.

ISBNs: 978-1-5460-3530-5 (hardcover) 978-1-5460-3529-9 (ebook)

Printed in the United States of America

LSC-C

10 9 8 7 6 5 4 3 2

CONTENTS

CONTENTS

EXPERIENCING ANGELIC VISITATIONS

There are two extraordinary experiences that I shall never forget. The first occurred in Virginia when I was beginning my full-time evangelistic ministry and the second occurred in Romania, when Jentezen Franklin and I were beginning a series of evangelistic crusades, following the collapse of Communism. Both involved angelic manifestations.

The year was 1977, in the hot summer month of June. I had just graduated from high school in Salem, Virginia, and was booking revivals in local churches, meeting pastors from churches across the state. Each year our denomination hosted a "camp meeting" in Roanoke, on a beautiful campground, under an open-air metal tabernacle that seated about 1,500 people. My heart was burning to reach people for Christ, and this zeal was being stoked by hours spent each day in prayer, study, and especially fasting. It was common for me to go for days without eating, in my earnest attempt to demonstrate to

God that my spiritual hunger exceeded my natural one. It was toward the weekend of the camp meeting that a strange and unexpected manifestation occurred.

I was the youngest evangelist serving on the altar committee, a position that required me to pray with and minister to the seekers praying in the altars, which were ten-foot-long wooden benches, about twelve inches wide, where people knelt for prayer. Drenched with perspiration, I had removed my black suit jacket and placed it on top of a five-foot cinderblock wall painted lime green at the front of the tabernacle. Nearby there was a concrete platform where the ministers, band, and choir sat facing the congregation. Standing to the far left side of the stage, I placed my hand on the top of the wall, and I noticed the room, with a door and a glass window, where the ushers counted the nightly offering.

Suddenly and without warning, I noticed the outline of a man who looked to be tall—definitely over six feet—forming on the cinderblock wall of the room, about a foot to the right of the wooden door. At first the person was flat in dimension, like a painting on the wall. However, within seconds, the form became three-dimensional, and I watched the entire "body" take on the curves of a person with a head, chest, arms, and feet. As I stood in shock, I realized this person was walking through the wall and toward me. The form became more detailed, and a sudden fear overcame me as I fell to the concrete floor on my knees and said, "No!" In retrospect, I have no idea why I said "no"—the word burst from my lips without thinking. Within about five seconds, I regained my composure, slowly standing and creeping back up to the wall, like a child playing hide-and-seek and sneaking around a corner to see if the person looking for him was still there. The person was gone. There was no trace. I felt a bit bewildered and angry with myself for saying "no" and ducking. That is, until later when I read in the Scriptures that most men who see an angelic manifestation experience fear, and the angel would immediately say, "Fear not" (Matt. 28:5; Luke 1:13, 2:10; Acts 27:24). Often the person seeing the angelic apparition would fall to the ground on their face (Dan. 8:17, 10:7; Rev 19:10).

I immediately told my father, who was near, a minister and man of great wisdom, and he said, "That was an angel of the Lord, and possibly an angel God has assigned to you to protect you as you travel…a ministering spirit" (Heb. 1:14). When I asked him why the angel had disappeared so quickly, he replied, "Angels move in the realm of faith and are offended at unbelief. When you said 'no,' it may have been out of fear, but it could be read as a rejection of what you were seeing. You didn't mean it as a rejection, but you should have reverently stood there in the fear of the Lord and followed through. There is no telling what would have occurred." I thought to myself, *Right. Stand there? That is easy for you to say, but I was afraid.*

Many years have passed, yet I can see this moment as though it occurred yesterday. Having had numerous angelic manifestations throughout my long ministry, I am certain Dad was correct. The Lord assigned an angel to me for my work. It may have been this same angel who made an important visit, years later, in Romania.

The Romanian Visitor

The fall of Communism had just occurred in Romania. I had accepted an invitation to minister there, and had invited my close friend, Jentezen Franklin, who was at the time serving as an evangelist in my same denomination.

Our first meeting was in a large auditorium in a major city, hosted by the pastor of a church. To our surprise, the other churches resisted attending the meeting (they perceived the event as competition instead of the kingdom working together), and someone tore down all of our posters that were placed throughout the city. The entire event was one of total confusion and discord. I remember returning to the hotel room one night very discouraged and thinking, *If all of these meetings are like this, this will be a disaster and no one will receive Christ or attend.* The power was out in much of the city. The hotel had a generator and I remember only one dull light in the parking lot that may as well have been a candle burning. The room had double beds and neither Jentezen nor I could sleep. Jentezen had never been away from his wife, and I was certainly missing mine and wishing I had not made this trip. The room was totally dark, but my watch had glowing hands that told me it was about three o'clock in the morning. Jentezen and I were actually conversing about missing our wives when suddenly, near the door, which was to the left in a narrow hallway, something moved.

At that moment that side of the room began to illuminate, to the point where I could see the pictures on the wall. Jentezen noticed the light and said, "Man, what's going on?"

I said, "I am not sure, but I feel a presence and it's coming from near the wall."

Within a few seconds, the entire room was lit up and we could see the furniture and the pictures, and most of all, we felt a supernatural holy presence. Once the entire room was visible to our eyes, with no natural or man-made lights on, we both felt the hair on our bodies rise up as standing between the beds we sensed the presence of an angelic visitor, whose holiness and vibrating energy was so strong that we both began shaking and crying at the same time. Wherever he moved throughout the room, the hair on the part of my body closest to him would stand up and I got goose bumps on my arms, legs, and the back of my neck. The electrically charged atmosphere and bright light stayed for what seemed to be between twenty and thirty minutes.

When the presence departed, the room returned to normal, the strange glow ceased, and we were both strengthened and felt at peace about the remaining part of the meeting. From the next day to the time we crossed the border days later to go back home, the buildings and auditoriums were packed and thousands received Christ! Jentezen and I both sensed that God was working behind the scenes and we had encountered an angel of the Lord—perhaps the very one that had first manifested when I was eighteen, the angel whom God had assigned to assist me in ministry during difficult seasons.

I realize there have been countless books written on the subject of angels. However, this book will detail specific and unique aspects of angelic visitations, assignments, and ministry purposes, which most pastors seldom cover. I will also reveal how these visitations will become more frequent and how we can and *should* believe God is sending angels to assist us throughout our life. The stories I will share are from my personal experiences, as well as from family and close friends. They are not embellished in any way. I have also included an appendix, answering twenty-one complex and, at times, controversial questions on angels and their ministry.

THIS SEASON OF
ANGELS

CHAPTER ONE

WE ARE ENTERING THE SEASON OF ANGELS

John 5:4 tells of a beautiful water source located near the sheep gate in Jerusalem where an angel bringing healing would occasionally manifest. John wrote that an angel appeared "at a certain season" (John 5:4). The word for "season" here in Greek is *kiaros*, a word used to indicate a specific season of opportunity that is also a set moment in time. The Scriptures teach us that there are "times and seasons" which God has placed within His own power (Acts 1:7). Prophetic signs indicate the world is entering the season identified as the "time of the end," which releases the most significant prophetic seasons since the birth, death, resurrection, and ascension of Christ. Biblically, there have been numerous prophetic seasons, including transitions that changed the world. When ignited, there is an increase in angelic visitations and angelic ministry. During tens of thousands of hours of reading, studying, and researching the Bible, I have been alerted to the importance of angels and their ministry to the human family.

The concept of angels ministering during specific set times is proven in Scripture in the book of Daniel. God's prophet in Babylon spent much of his life, during the seventy years of Jewish captivity, experiencing dreams or visions of future events, or interpreting the Babylonian king's own frightening dreams and visions, which in most instances revealed either the future of Babylon, or the progression of empires until the return of the Messiah (see Dan. 2).

When Daniel himself experienced these "other world revelations" that he could not understand, the angel Gabriel,

God's personal messenger assigned to carry and expose God's plans to his servants and handmaids on earth, became activated on direct assignments, explaining to Daniel amazing details related to the flow of worldwide events (see Dan. 7, 8, and 10–12). Perhaps the reason Daniel had numerous angelic encounters in Babylon is that prophetic seasons are of utmost importance to God, since Bible prophecy and the fulfillment of it is an essential key that proves both the existence and foreknowledge of God, and that the Bible is true. John also noted, "The testimony of Jesus is the spirit of prophecy" (Rev. 19:10). Old Testament prophecies detailing the Messiah were fulfilled in Christ, with 100 percent accuracy.

The importance of Biblical prophecy is significant for several reasons:

1. The fulfillment of end-time Biblical prophecy is an indicator that we are the generation living in the last days and a sign that Christ will return to earth to set up his kingdom in Jerusalem (Rev. 19:11–21).

2. The fulfillment of prophecy also indicates that Satan and his kingdom are running out of time. When Michael the archangel casts Satan out of heaven (Rev. 12), Satan will come down with "great wrath knowing that he has but a short time" (Rev. 12:12). Thus, prophecy is a time clock for man and for the spirit world.

3. The fulfillment of prophecy also indicates the imminent arrival of an upcoming cosmic battle in the second heaven between Michael's angels and Satan with his angels—the final cosmic conflict that initiates the greater tribulation

on earth and the soon return of Christ as the King of Kings over the nations before His visible return to earth (Rev. 12:7–10).

All these facts indicate that the kingdoms of light and darkness are both interested in the prophetic Scriptures. God is protective of His written Word to ensure that it comes to pass in the predetermined seasons, without delay or hindrance. This is one reason angels assist at times to ensure the fulfillment of prophecy and protect the outcome of each event within the specific set season. Angels understand that the ultimate desire of Satan would be to prove the spoken Word of God wrong, which would present God as unfaithful to His promises and make Him out as a liar. Of course, we know this will never happen, but a self-deceived person, at times, will attempt to convince themselves of things that will never be.

It reminds me of the days of Saddam Hussein, prior to the Gulf War. The wicked leader consulted psychics to receive a word of confirmation that he could defeat the United States military invasion and that he would come out victorious. We all know the true outcome. It was evident thousands of years ago, when the "false prophets" of Ahab—all 400—claimed that Ahab would win an upcoming battle. The truth was God had already predetermined beforehand the death of Ahab during the war, and when the battle was over, his followers buried the wicked king, leading, I am sure, to the "firing" of the 400 self-acclaimed prophets.

As the time of the end approaches, there will be increased angelic visitations, as prophetic seasons attract supernatural activity. When the "fullness of time was come" (Gal. 4:4), God sent forth his son to be born of a virgin to fulfill the birth, ministry, death, and resurrection prophecies of the future Messiah recorded throughout the Old Testament. When the set season arrived, the angelic activity increased consistently. The angel Gabriel announced John's birth to his father, Zacharias, and the same angel brought news to Mary of the coming birth of the Messiah, Jesus Christ. An angel appeared to Joseph in a dream and told him to take Mary for his wife. At the time of Christ's birth, angels announced the savior was born. These angelic visitations all transpired within eighteen months! Seasons of prophetic fulfillment indicate that the activity of angels among men will increase. Angels were activated to ensure that the birth of Christ went according to plan. The same occurred during Christ's ministry.

Entering Prophetic Seasons

As stated, Scripture provides the evidence that angelic visitations are increased during prophetic movements and seasons. A prophetic season is a set time in history when God's sovereign plans for individuals or nations, which have been predetermined in ages past in counsel rooms of heaven, are released upon the earth, fulfilling God's purposes.

In the Torah, we begin to see increased supernatural activity when Genesis introduces Abram, a godly man from Ur of Chaldea (the area of modern Iraq). God's plan was to separate Abram from his relatives in Ur, bring him into Canaan land (later called Israel), and through his future son Isaac, birth a new nation that would serve the true God and, eventually, maintain a godly lineage for the future Messiah, Jesus Christ.

Jewish tradition teaches that Abram's father, Terah, was an idol worshipper, yet Abram convinced him to depart from the city of Ur and join him in this new journey. The family traveled to Haran (located in Turkey). After Terah's death in Haran, Abram left the region and journeyed to Canaan land. The Lord began appearing to Abram, and each time, Abram built altars, offering sacrificial offerings to God (Gen. 12:7). Years later, after a brief war, "the Lord appeared to Abram in a vision" (Gen. 15:1), cutting a covenant with Abram which sealed God's promises to Abram that his descendants would inherit the land.

The first Biblically recorded angelic appearance was to Hagar, Sarah's personal handmaiden, whom Sarah, out of jealousy, expelled from her tent. The angel visited Hagar predicting she would birth a son named Ishmael whose descendants would in the future expand into a multitude. He would also be a "wild man" with a disposition to war against others (Gen. 16). After Ishmael's birth, "the Lord appeared to Abram and commanded him to walk perfect before Him as He planned to make Abram a great nation." This was when God changed his name from Abram (meaning "exalted father") to Abraham, which identified him as a father of a multitude. In Genesis 18, the Lord and "two men" (actually two angels) met with Abraham to confirm that within one year Sarah would conceive a son called Isaac. Genesis 19:1 tells us, "And there came two angels to Sodom." These angels appeared as men, unknown to the wicked men of Sodom who desired to gang-rape them, and were stopped when the two angels blinded the wicked men at Lot's door (Gen. 19:11). The next angelic messenger appeared when Abraham prepared to lay his son Isaac on the altar, and "the angel of the Lord called him out of heaven," to stop the process as God provided a ram for Isaac's substitute (Gen. 22:1–13).

The life of Abraham was filled with God encounters, appearing in visions and numerous angelic visitations. One reason for this increased angelic activity was to protect both Abraham and his wife, Sarah, from men who would unknowingly interrupt God's plan. On two occasions, two kings, Pharaoh, the king of Egypt (Gen. 12), and King Abimelech (Gen. 20), saw Sarah and desired to take her as a wife. Abraham was fearful the kings would kill him so he said Sarah was his sister, which made the kings pursue her. In both narratives, God intervened, by plaguing Pharaoh (Gen. 12:11–20) and by warning Abimelech in a dream that he "was a dead man" and not to touch Sarah (Gen. 20:1–18). In this dream, God marked Abraham as a "prophet." The king repented after the dream and sent Abraham and Sarah away. If any other man had taken Sarah as a wife, the divine plan to create a new nation called Israel, through Abraham's seed, would have been interrupted and ruined, requiring a new man and a new plan. Thus, both God and angels consistently protected the prophecies spoken to Abraham. When Abraham's son Isaac was a grown man, an angel of the Lord journeyed with Abraham's servant to connect him with the wife of God's will for Isaac (Gen. 24:40).

The second major sequence of visitations from both God and angels involved the life of Jacob, the grandson of Abraham and the son of Isaac. In Genesis 25, Jacob snatched his brother

Esau's birthright and tricked his father, Isaac, to receive Esau's firstborn blessing (Gen. 27). Esau, in anger, intended to kill Jacob. However, Jacob's mother, Rebekah, sensed the threat, and sent Jacob far from home into exile, to her brother Laban's home in Syria. There, Jacob lived twenty years, married Laban's daughters, Leah and Rachel, and was blessed with eleven sons (Benjamin was born later near Bethlehem). Angels were active from the beginning to the conclusion of Jacob's exile.

In a dramatic dream, shortly after fleeing from home to head into displacement, Jacob dreamed of a ladder reaching the top of heaven with angels ascending and descending to earth. God promised to return Jacob to the Promised Land, and in return, Jacob promised God a tenth (tithe) of his resources when the Lord fulfilled this promise (Gen. 28:12–22).

When the Lord released Jacob, an angel appeared and explained how God observed Laban's mistreatment of him. God blessed Jacob's labor because of the vow he made following the ladder dream twenty years ago. God's word was "leave Syria with your flocks and family and return to your home land" (Gen. 31:1–18). Laban was angry when he learned that Jacob slipped the family out secretly, leaving him unable to say good-bye to his daughters and his grandchildren. Laban pursued Jacob with the intention of harming him, until God appeared to warn him not to speak any evil concerning Jacob (Gen. 31:24). This was not the conclusion of angelic involvement in Jacob's life.

After leaving Laban and entering the covenant land of God, we read, "And Jacob went his way and the angels of God met him" (Gen. 32:1). Jacob saw and called them "God's hosts," meaning God's army. This angelic group was to provide assistance to

Jacob, knowing that Esau would show up with four hundred men (Gen. 32:1–6). Once Jacob entered the land that was promised to Abraham and Isaac, he was fearful of meeting Esau, knowing his brother could kill him and his entire family. Late at night, while alone, a "man" appeared to Jacob and he wrestled this man until sunrise. In reality, it was an angel in the form of a man. This "man" would not reveal his name to Jacob, and touched Jacob's hip, leaving the runaway patriarch with a permanent limp. We know this was an angel, as the Scripture says, "And Jacob called the name of the place Peniel, for I have seen God face to face, and my life is preserved" (Gen. 32:30). Prior to the birth of his last son, Benjamin, God appeared to Jacob to confirm the land covenant and to remind him that "a nation and a company of nations" would come from his sons. God reminded him that his name was no longer Jacob, but Israel (Gen. 35:9–13).

Had Jacob settled in Syria and not returned to the Promised Land, the nation of Israel would have never been formed. The Lord permitted Laban and his sons to turn against Jacob, forcing him to leave the country and return to the land promised to Abraham. At times, circumstances force us to make a decision in an opposite direction, which may move us away from our will, into the perfect will of God.

Angelic Activity Among the Prophets and Kings

Many of the Biblical prophets, including some exiled to Babylon, recorded numerous angelic visitations including visions of heaven where angels function in ministry. These visions are too numerous to list in this book and would require pages of just the Scripture references. However, a few noted examples are the visions of Isaiah (Isa. 6:1–3), Zechariah (Zech. 1–6), and Ezekiel (Ezek. 1 and 10), and throughout the book of Daniel.

Daniel lived through four leadership transitions: Kings Nebuchadnezzar, Belshazzar, Darius the Mede, and Cyrus, king of Persia. Daniel was about ninety when the Persians overtook Babylon. Based on the Scripture, the most intense angelic activity was before, during, and at the conclusion of the Jewish captivity in Babylon. King Nebuchadnezzar conducted three military campaigns against Israel, Judea, and Jerusalem, destroying the cities, the sacred Temple, and capturing Jews, leading them to Babylon as prisoners. A prophetic time limit was set for seventy years of captivity (Jer. 25:11). After the seventy years, when the time arrived for the Jews to return, God allowed the Medes and Persians, who were friendly to the Jews, to conquer Babylon, opening the door for the Jews to return to Judea and Jerusalem. One important Median leader was King Darius, and along with the Persian King Cyrus, he also gave Jews a release permit to rebuild the Temple. These new kings cleared the Jewish treasures to go out of the Babylonian houses, returning the sacred gold and silver temple vessels to the Jews.

In Daniel 10–12, the angel, whom scholars believe was Gabriel, spoke to Daniel, revealing nation alignments and future events. The angel told Daniel that he was under a divine mandate to stand with Darius, the king of the Medes, whose army had recently overthrown the Babylon king. The angel stated, "In the first year of Darius the Mede, even I stood to confirm and to strengthen him" (Dan. 11:1). The Hebrew word for "strengthen" is *ma'owz*, and refers to a fortified place, or in this instance a place of *defense*. Darius strategized how to defeat the Babylonian king, and during a late-night drunken party, where God etched a warning with his holy finger on the walls of the king's banquet hall, the intoxicated king and his kingdom fell (Dan. 5).

To understand the purpose of an angel strengthening Darius during the first year of his administration, we must note the prophecies of Jeremiah. Before this Persian invasion, Daniel was reading the scroll of Jeremiah and noted that the Jews would be in Babylonian captivity for seventy years (Jer. 25:11), and the seventy years were concluding. Prophecies indicated that the Jews would return to Israel, and rebuild the city and their sacred Temple. This return from exile would require a mass Jewish exodus from Babylonian captivity, which could *only occur* if the new Persian king (Darius) signed a legal decree of release and return. Historical records state that under Darius the Mede and Cyrus, king of Persia; the Jews did indeed receive a formal declaration securing their freedom and had their stolen temple treasures returned to Jerusalem. Publicly, the people observed the hand of Darius signing the declaration. However, behind the scene a mighty angel, for one year, assisted in Darius's smooth decision to ensure that the prophecy spoken by Jeremiah would be fulfilled.

Gabriel revealed, "I stood to confirm and to strengthen him" (Dan. 11:1). The NIV translates this as, "In the first year I took my stand to support and protect him." Scholars believe that the angel of the Lord protected Darius from men in his administration who would have convinced him *not* to allow the Jews to return, especially with their temple wealth. After the

Media-Persian army overthrew Babylon, Darius promoted Daniel to the first of three presidential positions, which angered some of the king's men. They encouraged the king to sign a law against prayer, yet Daniel ignored the decree, praying anyway, leading to his arrest and a death sentence by being thrown to hungry lions. Because God's angel shut the lions' mouths, Daniel was spared and released the following morning, unscratched (Dan. 6:19–22). Immediately, Darius sent a decree throughout the empire that Daniel's God was to be honored as the only true God (Dan. 6:25–28).

The lions' den narrative occurred shortly after Darius took the throne, which would have been his first year; the same year that the angel stood to strengthen and protect him. There is no Biblical record of Darius seeing this angel, as the angel was working behind the scenes in the spirit realm to ensure that the seventy years of captivity ended and the promise of rebuilding Jerusalem would begin. The return of the Jews was the second greatest prophetic event in Israel's ancient history, the first being the Exodus from Egypt 400 years after Abraham's promise (Gen. 15:13–14). During the Exodus, the angel of God's presence prepared the way for the people, and in Babylon, the angels Gabriel and Michael were both active in ensuring the prophecies came to pass. Gabriel confirmed this when he said, "But I will tell you what is noted in the Scripture of Truth. No one upholds me against these, except Michael your prince" (Dan. 10:20–21 NKJV).

The book of Daniel is a perfect example of angelic warfare during major prophetic seasons. Since we are living at the time of the end and the prophetic signs of Christ's return are now being fulfilled, this becomes a perfect season for increased angelic activity, in the world and in the Body of Christ!

There was a total of thirteen kings ruling in Babylon under the authority of Media and Persia, for about 200 years, until the conquest of the Greeks through Alexander the Great. What is fascinating is the angel of the Lord told Daniel that he would remain with the kings of Persia, until the prince of Grecia would come (Dan. 10:20). He also indicated he would "return to fight with the kings of Persia." Perhaps one reason the angel of the Lord was required for such a long assignment among the Persian kings is that one of the greatest dangers to the Jews would come in the same season, in the time of Esther. Haman, a wicked leader in the King of Persia's administration, would manipulate a decree for all Jews to be killed. It would be Esther's intervention that would stop this Satanic inspired plot (see the book of Esther).

The angel's message to Daniel is clear, that once the kings of Persia had completed their historic and prophetic rule (200 years), then the Greeks (Alexander the Great) would form an empire and be permitted to overtake Babylon, setting up their new global headquarters. Most of the angelic-demonic activity that occurred in upper regions and impacted the governments on the earth from 606 BC to 424 BC was in the territory of Babylon, Persia, and Jerusalem. In Daniel's time, the answers to his prayers were being disrupted over Babylon (Dan. 10). In Jerusalem, there was great opposition coming out of Samaria to prevent the Jews from rebuilding the city and the Temple, and Zechariah saw a vision of Satan himself standing on the right side of the altar to resist the High Priest from ministering (Zech. 3:1–3). Later in Persia, a plot was exposed that intended to have Jews in 127 provinces killed (see Esther). Satan was directly involved in these activities, by commissioning the prince spirits to hinder Daniel and block the angel's revelation; to inspire Haman and his sons to build ten gallows to hang the Jews in Persia; and to pay a visit on the temple mount in Jerusalem and personally resist Joshua the High Priest.

With this unusual angelic-demonic activity, each situation was overcome in a different manner. Daniel *persisted in prayer* for three weeks, until there was an angelic breakthrough. God raised up Esther to *expose the strategy* of Haman, preventing a mass genocide among the Jews. In Jerusalem, God *sent an angel* to resist and openly rebuke Satan. Each attack of the adversary in our lives has a specific counterstrategy we can tap into, to unlock the door of victory.

The Greatest Season of Angels

In the entire Bible, there is no other single time frame in which more angelic resources are put into place than from the conception to the ascension of Christ—a time frame estimated as thirty-five years. We must also note that increase in angelic activity initiates an increase in Satanic resistance, either by Satan himself or through his stronger prince spirits that operate over cities, nations, and governments.

For example, Satan wrestled the archangel Michael, hoping to seize the body of Moses prior to Israel crossing into the Promised Land (Jude 9). Satan provoked David to number Israel, bringing a swift judgment from God, prior to David purchasing the mountain where the holy Temple would be built (1 Chron. 21). Job was the greatest man in the East with tremendous influence and favor, yet Satan himself put a target on Job, to destroy all he had in an attempt to move Job to curse God and lose his integrity (see Job 1–2). When the Jews were rebuilding the Temple, the prophet Zechariah wrote that Satan stood at the right side of the altar near the Jewish high priest to resist him (Zech. 3:1–3). Satan no doubt motivated Herod to slay the infants two years and under in the territory in and around Bethlehem (Matt. 2:16), attempting to slay the mysterious Christ child future king that was born. At age thirty, Christ was tempted by Satan for forty days, another attempt to stop the redemptive plan of God (Matt. 4:1–10). When Christ spoke a powerful prophecy to Peter, the young apostle was targeted for a test, which unfolded the night of Christ's arrest. Jesus warned Peter, "Satan has desired you that he might sift you as wheat..." (Luke 22:31). Satan's kingdom receives a call to action when the forces of God are set in motion.

In the four gospels, there are two very specific and detailed times recorded in the ministry of Christ, where God commissioned angelic assistance to minister strength and encouragement to him: one at the beginning and the other at the conclusion of his ministry.

After Christ's baptism in water, the Holy Spirit directed him into the Judean wilderness for a forty-day mission of fasting and prayer. During the entire forty days, Satan tempted him. However, the strongest test was leveled at the conclusion of Christ's fast. Satan tempted Christ to turn rocks into bread to resolve His hunger; to jump from the highest wall (pinnacle) of the temple in Jerusalem and hit the ground unharmed; and to bow and worship him to obtain world power (see Matt. 4:1–8).

At the end of forty days, Christ was at His weakest physical moment. When Satan concluded the temptation, Luke wrote, "Satan left him for a season" (Luke 4:13). This word "season" refers to a future opportune time. Matthew noted that after the devil left him, "angels came and ministered unto him" (Matt. 4:11). The word "ministered" here comes from the same word used in the New Testament for a "deacon," a man in the church who attends to the needs of others. It is a word indicating that the angels were caring for the needs of Christ, which *may* have included providing food for him. I say this because during Israel's forty years in the wilderness, they were given manna, which is called "angels' food" (Ps. 78:25). Christ's forty days in the Judean wilderness was parallel to Israel's forty years in the Sinai desert, where food was unavailable and God provided manna. After the forty days of testing, Christ "hungered," and there is no record of when or how he was fed after the temptation, as he immediately returned to Galilee (Luke 4:18), which would be several days' walking. Did the angels bring heavenly manna for Christ, in the same manner that God provided for Israel, or the same way deacons fed those in need in the early church (Acts 6:1–4)?

The ministry of the angels far exceeded the influence and authority of Satan, as the strength of Satan was diminished when the spoken word of God (Heb. 4:12) cut through the voice of the adversary, and angels brought physical, emotional, and spiritual renewal to a weary Son, from His Heavenly Father.

Fast-forward forty-two months, to the conclusion of Christ's public ministry. In John 14, Christ alludes to his upcoming prayer time in the Garden of Gethsemane. He informed his disciples: "I will no longer talk much with you, for the ruler of this world is coming and has nothing in me" (John 14:30 NKJV).

The ruler of this world is Satan, whom Paul called "the god of this world" (2 Cor. 4:4), and also the "prince" of the power of the air (Eph. 2:2). In the garden, as Christ began interceding, his sweat became as great drops of blood (Luke 22:44). Medical research indicates this could only occur under the most extreme, stressful circumstances. The cause of this intense stress was the fact that Christ was becoming our sin substitute. The Father was placing the sins of mankind upon His Son, as Paul indicates that "he hath made him to be sin for us, who knew no sin; that we might be made the righteousness of God in him" (2 Cor. 5:21). In early times, on the Day of Atonement, the High Priest laid his hands upon the goats, ritually transferring Israel's sin to a sin substitute.

This transfer of man's sins to Christ was a mystery hidden from the foundation of the world and was unknown in the kingdom of Satan. Paul wrote that if the princes of this world would have known this redemption mystery, they would have "never crucified the Lord of glory" (1 Cor. 2:8). The ruler of this world, Satan, was present in the garden during Christ's extreme agony, and heard Christ praying to the Father asking if it were possible for the "cup" (of suffering) to pass from him. In the midst of emotional agony, Luke wrote, "And there appeared an angel unto him from heaven, strengthening him" (Luke 22:43). Later, when Christ stood to be arrested, Peter suddenly sliced off the ear of Malchus, servant of the High Priest. Jesus healed the man and told Peter to put his sword away (John 18:10–11). Then

Christ revealed this amazing fact: "Or do you think that I cannot now pray to My Father, and He will provide Me with more than twelve legions of angels?" (Matt. 26:53 NKJV).

Prior to this revelation in the garden, there is no mention of these legions of angelic deliverers. Why were there twelve legions? In 2 Kings 19:35, one angel walked through the army of Assyrians, slaying 185,000 in one night. In Christ's time, one Roman legion could be as many as 6,000 armed soldiers, making twelve legions as many as 72,000 angels. The number 12 is significant, as without Judas, there were 11 disciples, and with Christ, 12 persons were in the garden, implying that one legion could be assigned to each of the 12 men. Since angels can bring revelation from God to earth, this angel appearing to Christ in the midst of his mental and emotion pain would have revealed to him the *rescue option* provided as a backup plan should Christ choose to call off His Father's ultimate redemption plan, which prophetically included the scourging (Isa. 53:5) and the crucifixion (Ps. 22:16). Christ, however, rejected this optional plan and reminded Peter, "How then could the Scriptures be fulfilled, that this must happen?" (Matt. 26:54).

During his temptation in Luke 4, there was intense pressure on Christ's body (hunger), soul (mind), and spirit. The Garden of Gethsemane also affected all three aspects of the human nature: mind, body, and spirit. Satan was personally present during these two seasons of Christ's ministry as disobedience in either narrative and any wrong decision would have destroyed Christ's purpose and mankind's destiny. Christ's weakness required supernatural intervention brought to Him by angels who carry with them the divine presence of God. Peter wrote that there is "refreshing" that comes from the presence of the Lord (Acts 3:19), and angels bring this refreshing.

The birth of Christ was the greatest prophetic moment in world history, as without his birth, the initial Messianic prophecies would not be complete. Angels connected people (the shepherds) with God's plan, which was a divine setup. The ministry of Christ was a second wave of major prophetic activity, as his 42-month ministry brought to the forefront the fulfillment of numerous Old Testament prophecies proving he was the authentic Messiah anticipated by the Hebrew prophets. Angels were immediately commissioned prior to the public ministry of Christ, and also at the conclusion of his earthly ministry. As the final plans for mankind's redemption began unfolding, a personal ministering angel was provided for Christ to receive strength and encouragement.

As the ancient Biblical prophecies begin to transpire, the clash between the Kingdom of God and the kingdom of darkness intensifies, there is an unleashing of evil against men. However, God will release a multitude of angelic messengers for numerous assignments, including angels on "standby" preparing to release the major trumpet and vial judgments listed in the book of Revelation.

CHAPTER TWO

THE ANGEL WHO MINISTERS HEALING TO THE SICK

Now there is in Jerusalem by the Sheep Gate a pool, which is called in Hebrew Bethesda, having five porches. In these lay a great multitude of sick people, blind, lame, paralyzed, waiting for the moving of the water. For an angel went down at a certain time into the pool and stirred up the water; then whoever stepped in first, after the stirring of the water, was made well of whatever disease he had.

John 5:2–4

John is the only gospel writer to record this fascinating story of a healing angel. This angel "went down," which implies a special angel was sent "down" from heaven to this specific location for a single purpose: to bring healing to the first person who could discern the moving of the waters. This angel was commissioned to appear during a set time, or "season." In Jewish thought, Israel's special "seasons" were the seven "festivals" of Israel, called in Hebrew the *moadim*, or "appointed times" (Lev. 23). Some theologians suggest that this angel was sent to Jerusalem during one of Israel's seven festivals, likely Passover. The theory of Passover is significant. First, all men over twenty were required to attend this festival in Jerusalem, where Christ was at this time. He was mostly seen during the festivals. Second, the greatest mass healing on record occurred the night the Hebrew people ate the lamb in their homes at the first Passover (Exod. 12:5–10). The psalmist wrote that "God brought them forth... and not a feeble person was among them" (Ps. 105:37). The lamb's blood marking the outer doors protected the firstborns inside the home. However, by eating the pascal lamb, whatever infirmity or weakness was affecting their bodies was removed, resulting in an instant healing.

For the journey, the sick needed curing and the elderly needed strength. Therefore, Passover is both a redemptive and a healing festival. Apparently, the multitude of infirm and sick at the pool of Bethesda assembled, knowing the *season* when the healing angel would descend. There Christ healed a man, who church father Chrysostom suggested was blind, and therefore had difficulty seeing when the water was troubling. He could, however, hear the commotion of others moving once the water began stirring, but he was never able to move fast enough to be the first one in. His condition was some form of palsy, or part of his body was paralyzed, requiring others to assist him when he moved from one location to another, as indicated by "No man assisted him by putting him into the water."

There is also a church tradition of an angel being assigned as God's healing angel, whose name is Raphael. The early church father Origen (c. AD 185–254) wrote of certain assignments of angels and named Raphael as doing "the work of curing and healing." The name Raphael is unique for numerous reasons. God Himself revealed to the Israelites that if they followed Him in full obedience, He would not allow any Egyptian diseases to come upon them. He also gave His people a covenant name that when spoken identified Him as their healer, as in "For I am the Lord that healeth thee" (Exod. 15:26). The Hebrew word for "healeth" is *rapha'*, which means to mend something by stitching or, figuratively, to cure, heal, or make whole. The name Raphael conceals healing within his name, meaning "God heals." Raphael is considered (by tradition) to be one of the seven archangels in heaven, alongside Gabriel and Michael.

Raphael is alluded to in all three monotheistic religions: Judaism, Christianity, and Islam. The basis for some of the traditions is found in the writings of the noncanonical book of Tobit, which is accepted in the Catholic Church as deuterocanonical. In the story, Tobit asks Raphael to heal his eyes and to deliver his future daughter-in-law from an evil spirit. In Judaism, in the Book of Enoch (10:4–6), there are four archangels mentioned: Michael, Gabriel, Uriel, and Raphael, who allegedly assisted in binding the evil spirit Azazel under a desert mountain. The story of the angel bringing healing in John 5 caused some in the early church to connect this angel with Raphael.

It must be noted that throughout church history God has continued to perform miracles and heal the sick. The following statements by several early fathers confirm this:

For numberless demoniacs throughout the world and in your city, many of our Christian men exorcizing them in the name of Jesus Christ, who was crucified under Pontius Pilate, have healed, and do heal rendering helpless and driving the possessing devils out of men, though they could not be cured by all the other exorcists and those who used incantations and drugs. (Justin Martyr, AD 165, *Apologetics II*, Chapter 6)

Those who are in truth His disciples, receiving grace from Him, do in His name perform miracles; and they do truly cast out devils. Others still heal the sick by laying their hands on them and they are made whole. Yea, moreover, as I have said, the dead have even been raised up, and remained among us for many years. (Irenaeus, AD 200, *Hermetics*, Book I, Chapter 32)

And some give evidence of having received through their faith a marvelous power by the cures which they perform, invoking no other name over those who need their help than that of the God of all things, and of Jesus, along with a mention of His history. For by these means we too have seen many persons freed from grievous calamities and from other ills, which could be cured neither by men or devils. (Origen, AD 250, *Contra Celsum*, Book III, Chapter 24)

God's healing covenant never ceased and, even in the twentieth-century seasons of healing, was released upon the Body of Christ. During this healing season, godly men and women often reported sensing the presence or a manifestation of an angel of the Lord prior to receiving healing.

An Angel During the Healing Revival

Shortly after the reestablishment of Israel as a nation in May 1948, America entered a unique "season" of revival, which many full-gospel theologians identified as the "Restoration Revival" or the "Great Healing Revival." This revival continued strong for seven consecutive years (1948–1955), peaking around 1955. During this season, tens of thousands of believers in North America witnessed astonishing miracles, while sitting in giant tent cathedrals and large auditoriums. Gifted and anointed ministers would lay their hands upon the sick, offering a prayer of faith, and the audience would immediately see answers, as many seekers received healing through the "gifts of healing" or the "gift of the working of miracles" (see 1 Cor. 12:9–10). Many noted men such as T. L. Lowery, Oral Roberts, Morris Cerullo, R. W. Shambach, and my own father, Fred Stone, entered the ministry during this era of awakening.

One of the most noted and, at times, controversial figures

of the postwar healing revival, whose ministry extended from the 1940s until his death in the 1960s, was a minister named William Branham. Having met and fellowshipped with ministers over the years who personally knew and ministered with Branham, I have heard their amazing stories of the spiritual gift God imparted to Branham, a very humble man, to minister to the needs of the oppressed and the sick. In many cases, the miracles were so clear and dramatic that sinners came to believe upon Christ. He was called upon to pray for kings in Europe and in South Africa; after a major healing campaign, there was a parade of seven cattle trucks loaded with canes, crutches, and wheelchairs and thousands of healed people singing "Only Believe."

On one occasion, Branham was ministering in Texas and staying in the home of a pastor, who was to drive him to his next speaking engagement. As they were driving, Branham said, "The Lord told me that in twenty minutes we were going to see His glory manifest." Sure enough, twenty minutes later, they came upon a horrific car accident, where a child lay who was already pronounced dead. As they stopped the car and got out, the mother was hysterical and the police and emergency workers had surrounded the scene. Branham asked what happened and if he could pray. The officers replied no, but the mother demanded, "Let him pray!" The pastor watched as Branham laid his hands upon the dead child, prayed a fervent prayer of faith, and suddenly the child began moving, then became alert and was completely and instantly healed. This is one of hundreds of stories that could be told.

The most unusual manifestation, and the most criticized

by skeptics of Branham's ministry, was when an angel of the Lord that God assigned to his ministry would manifest during the public healing campaigns. He could discern the moment that the angelic messenger was present, and the results that followed his prayers—the stunning miracles—made it clear that the supernatural power of God was present to heal the people. Branham privately told close friends that when this angel was present in the auditorium, it would stand near the sick person and the area near them would illuminate. This was how he knew a healing miracle was coming. Just as an angel of the Lord appeared at the pool of Bethesda during a specific season, the miracles that followed were proof that the widely circulated story of a healing angel was true. Jesus said, "Believe me that I am in the Father, and the Father in me: or else believe me for the very works sake" (John 14:11).

Supernatural Healing of My Father

In my father Fred Stone's book, *Fire on the Altar*, he wrote about an event that occurred when he was pastor in Big Stone Gap, Virginia. I was a small child but can recall Dad being sent away to a hospital for a test. I knew something was wrong, but the family kept the details from us kids. Dad retells the story:

> I had my own experience with healing when I was about thirty-five years old. The problem started when I began to feel that I had been punched underneath my heart. Then I would become so physically weak that I had to lie down

and rest. Through an examination, the doctor located a tumor that he said was probably on the adrenal gland. He sent me to the University of Virginia Medical Center in Charlottesville for further tests.

Doctors at the University of Virginia performed medical tests for several days. On the sixth day, as I stood and looked out the window of my room on the fourth floor, I sensed that someone was watching me. I turned around but the other patient in the room was reading a newspaper, so I knew it wasn't him. When I turned back to look out the window, I saw a man outside standing in mid-air! I knew he had to be one of God's angels or some kind of manifestation of the Holy Spirit, because what human could be standing outside a fourth floor window in mid-air?

This man looked intently at me, from the top of my head down to my feet, as though he was examining me. Then he took a few steps and walked toward me. He had a spiritual body, and his body walked right through mine, and I actually felt my back to his. This lasted for a few seconds, then he stepped back through the window and once again faced me. He looked intently one more time before he turned and vanished. Immediately I felt energy from the top of my head to the bottom of my feet, and it was evident that God's supernatural power had touched my body. I left the room and walked down four flights of stairs to the lobby (which I could not do before). I walked around the lobby twice, and then I bolted up the same stairs to my room. When I got to the fourth floor I was not even out of breath.

As soon as I got back to my room, a nurse told me that I had a phone call from Ohio. It was my wife Juanita's brother-in-law, Frank Campbell, who attended a church in Mentor, Ohio. When I picked up the phone, Frank asked, "What happened at eight o'clock?" I told him the story. He said, "At eight o'clock our pastor read some scripture and started to preach. Then he stopped and asked me to stand. He asked if I had a brother in the ministry that was sick. I told him yes, and that you are in a hospital in Virginia undergoing tests for a tumor. The pastor called me forward and asked some of the men in the church to come pray for me on your behalf. The pastor anointed me with oil and the Spirit of God fell on the entire congregation and me. I asked the pastor if I could call you, and I am calling right now from his office in the church."

The next morning, the doctors told me that their previous tests detected deep internal bleeding and they would have to run some tests over again. I told them what happened the night before, even though I was certain they would be skeptical. I stayed for several more days while they ran the tests again, but no problem could be found. To this day, I have no trace of a tumor or internal bleeding.

My father passed away at age seventy-eight, and neither the tumor nor the bleeding ever returned. We discussed this miracle on several occasions and Dad would say, "The more I think about seeing what appeared to be a man that could move through a window, I believe this was a healing angel sent from the Lord." *Notice that the miracle occurred the same time the prayer was offered.* This reminded me of how the church prayed steadfastly when Peter was arrested and was scheduled to be executed after Passover. The same exact time the church was in prayer, God sent an angel of deliverance to free Peter from the prison (see Acts 12:1–11).

Biblical Methods of Healing

Paul wrote: "And the very God of peace sanctify you wholly; and I pray God your whole spirit and soul and body be preserved blameless unto the coming of our Lord Jesus Christ" (1 Thess. 5:23). God desires us to be both *holy* and *whole* (Heb.12:14; 1 Thess. 5:23). The common New Testament Greek word for "whole" is *holos,* meaning "altogether." It alludes to being healthy in body, soul, and spirit or, as we would say today, totally healthy. The "whole" man consists of the body (physical), soul (emotional), and spirit (spiritual). A person who is physically strong yet emotionally unstable is not completely whole. Someone who is spiritually strong yet physically sick to the point they cannot function is not totally whole. It is the will of God to preserve (to keep strong) our tripart being (body, soul, and spirit), preserved until the time our life is complete or until Christ returns—whichever comes first.

The Bible reveals a variety of methods employed to assist in healing. In the New Testament, Christ healed several blind men. He led one man outside the city and touched his eyes (Mark 8:23). On another occasion, he spat on the ground and smeared mud on a man's eyelids (John 9:6). In both instances, the men were cured. Christ would touch one person (Matt. 8:15), speak the word over another (Matt. 8:8), or command a person to put their faith in action to produce a miracle (Matt. 9:6). The methods varied, but the results were the same: People were healed.

There were about twenty people recorded in the four gospels who were healed in the ministry of Jesus (not counting raising the dead). Out of the twenty, there were some whose problem was caused by a spirit (Luke 4:33, 9:42, 13:11, etc.), others who needed a deliverance, and some who required a miraculous cure.

There are four main branches of the healing tree that are found in the New Testament:

1. Miracles that occur through *signs and wonders* (Heb. 2:40)
2. Miracles that occur because of an *anointing* (Acts 10:38)
3. Miracles that occur through a *deliverance* (Luke 4:18)
4. Miracles that occur by accepting the *atonement of Christ* (1 Pet. 2:24)

Using the Scripture as our guide, there are four New Testament (New Covenant) methods used to bring healing. While there are many Scriptures to back up each method, I will only list one reference:

1. The method of laying on of hands (Mark 16:18)
2. The method of the anointing with oil (James 5:14–15)
3. The operation of the gifts of healing and working of miracles (1 Cor. 12:7–10)
4. The power of the spoken Word (Ps. 107:20)

Christ, his disciples, and the New Testament apostles would lay their hands upon the sick to impart healing (Mark 16:18). According to Mark 5:30, those who exercised faith could literally feel the healing "virtue" (power) enter their bodies (Mark 5:30). Numerous examples are found where the sick were cured through the ministry of laying on of hands. Laying on of hands is also a basic doctrine in the Christian Church (Heb. 6:2). Using this method, certain spiritual gifts are also transferable (2 Tim. 1:6).

James (5:14–15) instructed the elders in the church to anoint the sick with oil: "Is any sick among you? let him call for the elders of the church; and let them pray over him, anointing him with oil in the name of the Lord: And the prayer of faith shall save the sick, and the Lord shall raise him up; and if he has committed sins, they shall be forgiven him."

Oil is a symbol of the anointing of the Holy Spirit. Under the Old Covenant, when olive oil was poured upon the heads of the future kings, the Spirit of the Lord would come upon them (1 Sam. 16:13). It is the anointing of the Holy Spirit that "breaks the yoke" of bondage (Isa. 10:27). In the early church, the elders (the older and spiritually mature men in the congregation) would pray over the sick and anoint them with oil. If the prayer was offered "with faith," the sick would be healed. The healed person was then required to confess their faults one to another, and to pray for others.

"Confess your faults one to another, and pray one for another, that ye may be healed. The effectual fervent prayer of a righteous man availeth much" (James 5:16). Notice how the Scripture connects healing and forgiveness. This passage teaches the need to confess one's faults, which refers to making amends with another believer if there has been a division in the church.

The third method of New Covenant healing is through a manifestation of the gifts of healing and working of miracles as found in 1 Corinthians 12:7–10: "For to one is given by the Spirit the word of wisdom; to another the word of knowledge by the same Spirit; to another faith by the same Spirit; to another the gifts of healing by the same Spirit. To another the working of miracles…" These gifts are a supernatural impartation from the Holy Spirit, providing the ability to pray for the sick and afflicted, releasing a manifestation of God's miraculous power. Throughout history, God has used the prayers of righteous men and women to experience miracles of answered prayer, including miracles of healing (James 5:16).

The fourth method comes by "speaking the Word." There are several New Testament examples where Christ simply spoke the word to bring healing to the infirm. A centurion had a sick servant at home and came to Christ, saying, "Speak the word only and my servant shall be healed" (Matt. 8:8). The man's servant was cured the very moment Christ spoke the healing word (Matt. 8:13). Jesus said this was the greatest level of faith, to have faith in the power of the spoken word (Matt. 8:10).

At times a person will stand in place on behalf of another person, as my dad's brother-in-law did, as noted in the previous story. A prayer of faith is offered in the name of the Lord on behalf of the person who is suffering. This agrees with Psalms 107:20: "He sent his word, and healed them, and delivered them from their destructions." Based upon the John 5 narrative, we must add the possibility of God permitting an angel of healing to bring His healing power to a person in need of a miracle.

When asking for healing, we are to ask God in the name of the Lord Jesus Christ for His healing power to manifest in our mind, body, or spirit—wherever the healing is needed. James said the elders of the church should anoint the sick with oil in the name of the Lord, praying a prayer of faith for the sick to be cured (James 5:14–15). Angels of healing are activated under the authority and commandment of the Lord and we should *never pray directly to any angel*. However, even if we do not need a physical healing, we can petition God to provide supernatural strength from angels, as part of their ministry is to strengthen those who are in spiritual battles. This passage in Daniel affirms this fact:

> And suddenly, one having the likeness of the sons of men touched my lips; then I opened my mouth and spoke, saying to him who stood before me, "My lord, because of the vision my sorrows have overwhelmed me, and I have retained no strength. For how can this servant of my lord talk with you, my lord? As for me, no strength remains in me now, nor is any breath left in me." Then again, the one having the likeness of a man touched me and strengthened me. And he said, "O man greatly beloved, fear not! Peace be to you; be strong, yes, be strong!" So when he spoke to me I was strengthened, and said, "Let my lord speak, for you have strengthened me." (Daniel 10:16–19 (NKJV)

Angels continually dwell in God's presence; thus when they enter the earthly realm, the presence of God can be perceived if the believer is sensitive to spiritual atmospheres. Angels can and do strengthen us, and new covenant believers can ask the Lord to commission angels to assist us in strength and help us when needed.

CHAPTER THREE

ANGELS ASSIGNED TO BRING HEAVENLY REVELATIONS TO EARTH

In both the Old and the New Testaments, there is one noted angel, who during a 600-year time frame made personal visits to the Hebrew prophet Daniel in Babylon, to a Jewish priest at Jerusalem's Temple, and to a young virgin named Mary living in Nazareth. This angel is Gabriel, whose name means "Man of God." He is one of two angels mentioned by name in Scripture, the other being Michael the archangel (Dan. 12:1; Jude 9). Clearly, Michael is the highest-ranking angel in authority who also commands an army of angels (Rev. 12:7). At Moses' death, Satan strategized to seize possession of his corpse. Not only did God send Michael to resist and rebuke Satan, but after Satan departed, God Himself scooped up the remains of Moses, placing Israel's greatest prophet in a private burial plot that remains a secret to this day (Deut. 34:6; Jude 9).

In a more dramatic face-to-face conflict, the prophet Daniel sought God for the interpretation of a strange vision he had received. However, the heavens were like cold brass. Daniel and his companions normally were a "one-day breakthrough" group—whether at the fiery furnace or the lions' den, when they ended up in dangerous places with death breathing down their necks, there an instantaneous deliverance always occurred. In the Daniel 10 narrative, three weeks of prayer and fasting had not penetrated the barrier that blocked the understanding that Daniel was seeking.

The issue was not that God was too busy to hear Daniel's prayer, or that God was testing him—He would just send the answer when He was good and ready. The problem was not found in the third heavenly realm, where God and angels join for heavenly counsels, nor was there some iniquity in Daniel's heart that could hinder his prayer (Ps. 66:18), as Daniel was a godly man. The standstill was headquartered in the second heaven, above Babylon, where two strong spirits—a demonic prince of Persia and God's special messenger (believed to be Gabriel)—were in a face-off where the powerful evil prince spirit attempted to restrain righteousness. His demonic interference seemed temporarily stronger, as it restrained God's messenger in the upper heaven from breaking through the earth's atmosphere. God observed this struggle of dueling angels and released His "secret weapon," who was on standby, waiting to fly like a rocket to the scene of struggle: Michael the archangel.

Michael entered the cosmic wrestling match and, using his superior authority, seized control of the demonic prince of Persia, immediately releasing Gabriel, God's messenger of revelation, to complete the assignment to which he was appointed. God's original plan was to release this information to Daniel on the first day of his prayer. The angel told Daniel:

> Do not fear, Daniel, for from the first day that you set your heart to understand, and to humble yourself before your God, your words were heard; and I have come because of your words. But the prince of the kingdom of Persia withstood me twenty-one days; and behold, Michael, one of the chief princes, came to help me, for I had been left alone there with the kings of Persia. Now I have come to make you understand what will happen to your people in the latter days, for the vision refers to many days yet to come. (Daniel 10:12–14 NKJV)

As God's angelic messenger suddenly entered Daniel's prayer room, the prophet fell to the ground and the angel responded, "I have come for your words." These words were Daniel's prayer request to receive complete and perfect understanding of a mysterious vision (Dan. 10:1–2).

On two occasions, the angel Gabriel is mentioned by name as bringing prophetic understanding concerning the future to Daniel. The first is in Daniel 8, in which Gabriel reveals the animal symbolism seen in Daniel's vision and explains how each animal represents a future empire. A voice coming from the banks of the Ulai River tells Gabriel to "make this man to understand the vision" (Dan. 8:16). In Gabriel's second appearance, he was seen by Daniel after the Medes and Persians overtook Babylon in a secret invasion. Daniel was reading the scroll of Jeremiah, which predicted that the Jews would return from Babylon after seventy years (Jer. 25:11, 29:10). Daniel was boldly repenting for Israel's sins and questioned if God would keep the promise of seventy years' captivity and transition the Jews from Babylon back to Jerusalem. To his amazement, Gabriel revealed a previously unknown prophetic cycle that would involve, not seventy years, but seven times seventy weeks (490 years). This revelation of a new time required Gabriel to explain the detailed division of the seventy weeks. We read:

Now while I was speaking, praying, and confessing my sin and the sin of my people Israel, and presenting my supplication before the LORD my God for the holy mountain of my God, yes, while I was speaking in prayer, the man Gabriel, whom I had seen in the vision at the beginning, being caused to fly swiftly, reached me about the time of the evening offering. And he informed me and talked with me, and said, "O Daniel, I have now come forth to give you skill to understand. At the beginning of your supplications the command went out, and I have come to tell you for you are greatly beloved; therefore, consider the matter, and understand the vision." (Daniel 9:20–23 NKJV)

An interesting insight is in the sentence "At the beginning of your supplications the command went out, and I have come to tell you…" This phrase conceals a dynamic *prayer revelation*. The supplication, which alludes to Daniel's prayer request, ascended from Babylon to God's throne without any time delay or demonic resistance. God's response was immediate and the phrase "the command went out" refers to God's direct instruction to bring the answers Daniel was praying for. This indicates that God commands angels to bring certain messages and insights at specific times. Gabriel's urgency to inform the prophet is noted as he began to "fly swiftly," to Daniel's prayer location in Babylon.

In the English translation of the King James Bible, the word "fly" is found twenty-two times, and five different Hebrew words are used. The common word means "to fly like a bird." The word "fly" used in this Daniel reference is *ya'aph* and has a root that refers to being "wearisome, as by flight." This word indicated that as God's angels were moving toward Daniel, there was a conflict that would create a wearisome situation in the movement of the angel. Just as a human would become weary from nonstop battle day after day, the angel was in a literal wrestling match for three weeks in the heavenly realm.

The prophetic revelations that Gabriel released to Daniel in chapter 11 concerning the future are so precise and detailed that only God Himself could have aligned future events that came to pass in history. Why is Gabriel selected as God's primary messenger to announce important revelations to specific individuals? The answer is found in an appearance of Gabriel from the New Testament.

Gabriel Reveals God's Hidden Plan

Luke expounds on two narratives in which Gabriel is directly involved in explaining the conception of two sons: John the Baptist and Jesus. The first story unfolds at the Temple in Jerusalem, where the priest Zacharias is chosen to burn incense on the golden altar in the Holy Place, only to be interrupted by an unexpected visitor who is standing at the right side of the altar, which is traditionally the side reserved for God Himself. The angel says, "I am Gabriel that stands in the presence of God" (Luke 1:19). As Gabriel stands in God's presence, he is aware of God's plans, strategies, and prophetic purposes on earth. Gabriel knows the secrets of heaven, the mysteries of God, the strategies of angelic assignments determined in the heavenly counsels and reported those plans to men on earth throughout Biblical history. Such was the case with Zacharias. Gabriel knew that Zacharias and his wife had prayed for a son, and God had heard their prayer. Gabriel released the details: Zacharias would have a son named John (Luke 1:13), and the child would be filled with the Spirit from his mother's womb, and he would minister in the spirit of Elijah to prepare the way for the Messiah (Luke 1:15–17).

Gabriel's knowledge of this information was not "new" to him, as the Old Testament prophets had penned predictions of John's mission in Isaiah 40:3: "The voice of one crying in the wilderness to prepare the way of the Lord." Four hundred years before John's birth, Malachi wrote in Malachi 3:1 to reaffirm that God would send a messenger to prepare the way of the Lord. This was John the Baptist's assignment. The predictions were set but the fulfillment was in the future, hundreds of years before both Isaiah and Malachi. When the time did arrive, Gabriel was sent to the future parents to give the additional details known only to heaven.

Six months later, Gabriel's most significant revelation was disclosed in the tiny town of Nazareth, a village community where some scholars believe perhaps thirty families lived. Gabriel visited Nazareth to bring a message that would be repeated in every generation, till this day. Gabriel appeared to a teenage virgin named Mary, indicating that she would supernaturally conceive the seed of God through the Holy Spirit's power. Her son, Jesus, would be called the Son of God and become the world's savior (Luke 1:31–33). The predictions spoken by Gabriel were fulfilled in detail through the ministry of John and Christ.

Angels Bringing Illumination

During the Old Testament dispensation, angels were needed in giving instruction and direction to God's people. The word "angel" (singular) is mentioned 201 times in 192 verses in the

Bible, with 104 of those references found in the Old Testament. Angels traveled from the upper celestial realm with time-sensitive and life-changing information, giving direction and, at times, warnings, to patriarchs, prophets, and holy priests. It must be remembered that there was no law or written word from God, from the time of Adam until Moses received the Torah (five books) on Mount Sinai—a stretch of 2,500 years. When a "word from God" was required, the message came through a spiritual dream or vision, a spoken word of inspiration, or through an angelic visitation.

Prior to Moses penning the Torah, visitations from angels were necessary to bring God's word and will to men. Mount Sinai is the sacred mountain where God descended to give Moses the law and the commandments. David wrote, "The chariots of God are twenty thousand, even thousands of angels; the Lord is among them, as Sinai, in the holy place" (Ps. 68:17). The giving of God's law to Israel was so important that angels surrounded Mount Sinai as God's Word was burned into the stone tablets. The gospel is a curiosity to the spiritual realm as noted in the verse "angels desire to look into" (1 Pet. 1:12). Hebrews 2:2 says, "For the word spoken by the angels was steadfast..." True angels will always agree with the revealed, written Word of God.

False Angels of Revelation

A firm warning should be noted here. Because the Jews in Paul's day knew how significant the ministry of angels was in bringing God's word to earth, Paul also gave believers cautionary advice when he wrote: "But even if we, or an angel from heaven, preach any other gospel to you than what we have preached to you, let him be accursed" (Gal. 1:8 NKJV).

Why would Paul warn of angels preaching another gospel? In context, his warning covered the danger of false prophets entering the church, introducing new revelations contrary to the pure gospel of Christ. Some heretical doctrines in Paul's day included the teaching that Jesus was an angel and not a man, that Christ was not the Son of God, or that He was only a mortal who had not preexisted with God.

During the past 1,500 years, two noted religions have made claims to be birthed through spiritual revelations given by angels to their founders. The main challenge to these theories is that both of these religions teach certain doctrines or concepts that are contrary to the sacred Word of God.

The first is Islam, whose founder, Muhammad, alleged that the angel Gabriel appeared to him, bringing him new spiritual revelations for those living in Arabia. At first, Muhammad appeared to be friendly toward Jews and Christians, until they rejected his claim as a prophet. The sayings of Muhammad are written in Islam's main book, the Quran. There are verses in the Quran that agree with the Scripture, such as Mary being a virgin and Jesus being conceived through divine means. Islam also accepts Jesus as a prophet. However, the significant difference between Biblical Christianity and Islam is that, according to the angel's message in the Quran, Jesus is not the Son of God as "Allah (God) cannot begat a son." Whatever possible angelic manifestation Muhammad received, the doctrine of Jesus not being the Son of God does not agree with the message of Gabriel, who appeared to Mary and declared that Jesus would be "called the Son of God" (Luke 1:35). The answer most Muslims give to explain this contradiction is that the Jews and the Christians changed the Bible to make it read in agreement with their doctrine. There are numerous theological and historical differences in certain Islamic beliefs and the Scripture.

The second major religion, headquartered in the United States, claims that its sacred book, the Book of Mormon, was translated from gold plates hidden in the Hill Cumorah by an angel named Moroni in New York State. The angel allegedly led Joseph Smith to the concealed location, and Smith peered through two stones to interpret the ancient language on the plates identified as "reformed Egyptian," now extinct. The message was printed in the Book of Mormon and claims that two groups of people migrated to America before the time of Christ and eventually extinguished each other in battle.

There are many good, moral Mormons who have a love for God. However, the question remains: Was the Book of Mormon inspired, or is it a man-made novel that was marketed as a divine revelation? There are numerous verses in the Book of Mormon that contradict proven Biblical doctrines, all of which have been exposed by knowledgeable evangelical scholars. Finally, the angel of revelation who supposedly appeared to Joseph Smith was not an angel of the Lord with some new revelation—I believe this is an example of what Paul alluded to when he warned believers not to heed the words of any angel who would bring a new or another gospel.

The Purpose for Any Revelation

Any angel sent from God never contradicts the Holy Scriptures. However, Paul taught that Satan can "transform himself as an angel of light," thus converting his ministers into "ministers of righteousness." The context here is Paul warning the church of false apostles and deceitful workers infiltrating the church at Corinth (see 2 Cor. 11:13–15).

The purpose of "angelic revelation," especially in the New Testament, is often to bring either a warning of coming danger or some type of necessary instruction related to God's will (for more information, see the next chapter). For any believer, the most important path in our journey is where God's perfect will leads us. In this dispensation, we are blessed to have the Holy Spirit working as our helper (Rom. 8:26), quickening our understanding toward God's will. The Word of God is His complete revelation to mankind, revealing future events and the plan of redemption through the Messiah, Jesus Christ. Angels were involved in the process and continue to be involved in ministering to the people of God.

CHAPTER FOUR

WHEN ANGELS APPEAR IN DREAMS AND VISIONS

The twenty-seven New Testament books are filled with unique stories of angels bringing instructions and warnings through dreams or visions. Most people experience dreams during their sleep and a few have experienced visions. A vision differs from a dream. If a person dreams, they may not be aware they are actually sleeping or in a dream state, until they awaken. A vision, however, presents itself in a clear, full-color, and three-dimensional way and is so well defined, it is as though you're awake and your eyes are open. The details of a vision are precise, and your five senses are in full operation.

At the same time, dreams have changed the outcome of major events. When Joseph was plotting to separate from Mary after discovering she was pregnant, an unnamed angel appeared to him in a dream revealing God's purpose for Mary and the child, who would be the "Son of God." In contemporary times, an engaged man having such a dramatic dream would have written it off as an overactive imagination or some bad food being digested too late at night. Joseph, however, followed the angel's direction, and took Mary for his wife (Matt. 1:20–25).

Joseph's second angelic dream was after the Christ child was born. Herod, the jealous ruler of Judea, was threatened by the infant Christ's destiny to be king. In an envious rage, Herod lost control and went on a killing rampage, ordering soldiers to slay all infants under two years of age in and around Bethlehem. This death decree placed Christ in the target of Herod's death squad, initiating God to set up an escape strategy for the holy family. In a dream, an angel of God told Joseph to take the young child and His mother to Egypt (Matt. 2:13–15).

It would be months later when a third directional dream was revealed to Joseph, once again by an angel of the Lord, telling him to bring the family back to Israel, as Herod was now dead and his plot was no longer a threat (Matt. 2:19–21). This angelic command to return fulfilled a prophecy in Hosea 11:1: "Out of Egypt I have called my son."

Fulfilling the Words of the Prophets

In each of these three narratives involving Joseph, the Old Testament prophets pierced the veil of the future. Isaiah knew the Messiah would be born of a virgin (Isa. 7:14); Hosea said God's "son" would be called out of Egypt (Hosea 11:1); and when the family departed from Egypt with the intent of living in Judea, Joseph instead moved to Nazareth in Galilee, which fulfilled numerous prophecies, revealing that Galilee would produce a light for the Gentiles (Isa. 11:10; 49:6). Joseph's obedience to the angelic dreams is to be commended, as it placed Christ in the right place at the right time and protected Him from a premature death.

The ministry of angels was activated during the formation and growth of the early church. At the time of the early acts of the apostles (recorded in the book of Acts), the New Testament we have today was not written and compiled into one book. The New Testament canon would later be approved by the church counsels to be made into twenty-seven books. In Acts, angelic activity is consistent as angels are seen delivering the apostles, warning individuals in dreams, and connecting people for the Kingdom of God.

Angels Connect People

Angels have used visions and dreams to assist in connecting people together for Kingdom purposes. In Acts 10, an Italian centurion was praying when an angel in "bright clothing" (Acts 10:39) appeared and gave him the good news that his prayers and charitable contributions had come before God as a memorial (Acts 10:4). This angel was in the process of connecting two men—a Gentile named Cornelius and a Jewish apostle, Simon Peter. At this time in history, devout Jews had no dealings whatsoever with Gentiles. Thus, it required a supernatural event or divine encounter to connect these two opposing ethnic groups. Cornelius was instructed to send men to Joppa and inquire about a man named Simon Peter who resided in the house of Simon the Tanner near the Sea (Acts 10:30–32). Notice the details given by the angel: Peter's location in Joppa; the owner of the house where Peter was staying, a man named "Simon" who was "a tanner"; the home being situated near the (Mediterranean) Sea. Joppa was a large seaport city, and when these men journeyed to the region, they needed such details, including the man who was assigned to bring Cornelius a gospel message: "Simon whose surname is Peter" (Acts 10:5).

In order to prepare Peter to minister to these Gentiles, he experienced a strange vision, a sort of "illustrated message," in which God informed him that what He called clean, Peter should receive. Moments later a knock on the door confirmed the meaning of the vision and Peter began a journey into new territory that would alter the course of spiritual history, and would introduce the Gentiles into the redemptive covenant (Acts 10:10–21).

Based upon Jewish cultural restrictions of fellowshipping with Gentiles, had an early prophet in the church "prophesied" to Peter that God chose him to meet and preach to this Gentile family, Peter would have likely rejected the idea. The details from the angel were so precise and confirmed by Peter's own spiritual vision that he understood the visit and his obedience fulfilled the sovereign plan of God.

Angels Revealing the Will of God

A night vision that I experienced years ago set the course for our worldwide ministry that today is reaching millions. At the time, in 1988, Pam and I were traveling the nation conducting local revivals in churches. My vision occurred in the month of July during a four-week tent revival in Leeds, Alabama.

Early one morning while in a deep sleep, I suddenly found myself in a full-color, three-dimensional vision. I was standing at the bottom of a set of old concrete steps that led to the top of a small hill, where I observed a tall metal television tower with small round satellite dishes attached midway up the structure. To the left side, I clearly saw a man, about six feet four inches tall, dressed in a black suit, a white shirt, and a dark tie. A strange feeling that I would describe as a "holy awe" settled over me. The man lifted his left hand to the metal tower, pointing his index finger to the dishes, then said to me, "If you will do these three things, then God will give you this." He proceeded to give me three direct instructions, including one that was personal and two that emphasized the importance of my total obedience to God in the ministry.

When the vision faded, I knew by inner revelation that the tower was somehow linked with television and the satellite dishes would carry my messages around the world. Yet I did not own any type of video or television equipment, much less cameras or a studio. I told this vision to only a few close friends and hid the information in my heart. Shortly thereafter, we purchased a 7,000-square-foot building to expand our outreach ministry, and Dorothy and Russell Spalding built our first studio there to tape prophecy videos. In two years, our growth required us to build a much larger facility and acquire land for future development. After weeks of searching, one day I came across eighteen empty acres, and while walking through the tall grass, I was stunned to come across the exact concrete steps leading up the knoll that I saw in the 1988 vision. On this property now sits the Voice of Evangelism headquarters and the studio for producing our weekly *Manna-fest* telecast. The place where the man stood in the vision is today the place where the gospel is being preached and heard around the world.

The "man" in the vision always intrigued me. Who was he? How did he have such detailed future information that came to pass? When I told my father about the vision, he asked me, "How did the man address you, by your name, or did he just reveal the three points to you?"

I said, "I remember he did not call me Perry, but he said, 'Son.'"

Dad replied, "Every time the Lord has ever spoken to me, he called me 'son' and not 'Fred.'" In Scripture, the same was true when many prophets in the Bible received a word from God. Ezekiel is called "son of man" ninety-two times. Both Dad and I believed that the person in the vision was an angel in the form of a man sent to earth to reveal what would occur in the future of the ministry, as the information was an unknown plan and a revelation directly from God.

In over forty years of ministry, I have never experienced a dream or vision in which I saw an angel in the form as recorded in the Scripture. Isaiah in his vision saw God's throne room surrounded with angelic beings worshipping the Almighty. Identified as "seraphim," each had six wings, three on each side, with two covering their eyes, two their feet, and two used for flying (Isa. 6:2–3). Their ministry is to worship God, reminding all heavenly creatures that God is "Holy" (Isa. 6:3). In Revelation, John describes four "beasts," or living creatures, surrounding God's throne with the faces of an ox, a lion, an eagle, and a man (Rev. 4:7). The assignment of these unique heavenly creatures is the same as the seraphim, to worship and announce the holiness of the Lord (Rev. 4:8).

In many angelic visions, especially in Daniel, the angelic messenger takes on the appearance of a man (with head, arms, legs, and bodily features), but the angel's face flashes like lightning and his eyes appear as fire with feet similar to bright polished brass (Dan. 10:6). Angels called cherubim have dual faces, that of a man and a lion with feet similar to the feet of calves (see Ezek. 1 and 10).

However, in the days of the patriarchs, angels often appeared in human form. One example is when Jacob was left alone and he "wrestled a man...to the breaking of day" (Gen. 32:24). This "man" however, proved to be an angel of the Lord who, at the conclusion of the wrestling match, put a blessing on Jacob, changing his name to Israel. Afterward we read: "And Jacob called the name of the place Peniel: for I have seen God face to face, and my life is preserved" (Gen. 32:30).

A similar incident occurred in the life of Abraham. One afternoon, this godly patriarch looked up from his tent door to see two men approaching. After a generous meal, and a series of negotiations concerning the possible destruction of Sodom, the Lord instructed the two "men" accompanying him to journey to Sodom to confirm if ten righteous individuals remained among the wicked in the city (Gen. 18). These two men were actually angels taking on human form and were not recognized by the population in Sodom (Gen. 19). Only when these two strangers supernaturally blinded the men of Sodom at the door of Lot's house to prevent them from violently raping Lot, did they realize they were dealing with two beings from another world.

If an angel appears in a dream, don't necessarily expect to see a glowing creature in white with large feathers like wings flapping in your face. This is the common image of an angel, as often displayed on canvas oil paintings, in older Bible etchings, and in modern movies. Angels in their spirit bodies can have wings (Isa. 6:2–3), but in human appearance, they take the form of men.

In a dream, an angel can appear in the form of a normal-looking man. It is important to note several things:

1. How does the "person" address you in the dream or vision—as "son" or "daughter" or by your name? Angels will use both "son" and "daughter" and the common name of the person.

2. What information is revealed? Is it a direct warning or a revelation of what will occur in the near future?

3. Is the revelation given in line with the Word of God? If not, it should not be feared, revered, or accepted, as angels always "harken to the voice of God's word" (Ps. 103:20).

Some theologians suggest that there is no need for any type of "revelation," since we have the Scriptures, which is basically true. However, I have noted there are many important decisions that must be made in life that can only be revealed through prayer and revelation. The Bible teaches that we should marry a believer, but only by "revelation" (understanding something unknown) can you know who is the right person. We are told that God will bless the works of our hands; however, the Bible never says where to live and work. This must be made known by the leading of the Holy Spirit through prayer. Being at the right place at the right time enables a person to meet others (or kingdom connections) that are assigned to open doors for your future. The Bible certainly reveals how to morally and spiritually live, how to treat others, and how to respond in negative situations. It does not tell you how many children you should have as this is made known as God directs the formation of your family.

Paul told the church at Corinth he would speak by "revelation, knowledge, prophesying, or by doctrine" (1 Cor. 14:6).

Paul prayed the church would receive the "spirit of wisdom and revelation in the knowledge of him" (Eph. 1:17). In Acts 8, Phillip was preaching in Samaria when an angel of the Lord spoke to him to travel to Gaza (ninety-four miles away), where Phillip met an Ethiopian eunuch who was under Queen Candace's authority, who was converted to Christ and baptized in water (Acts 8:26–40). This conversion was significant as many of the Christians in Ethiopia trace their roots to this one man who tradition says assisted in the spread of Christianity in the region. In Acts 27, the vessel in which Paul was sailing hit a storm lasting fourteen days and the ship began falling apart. An angel of the Lord appeared at night giving a threefold revelation:

1. The ship would be destroyed but none of the men onboard would die (Acts 27:22).
2. Paul would be cast upon an island for a brief time (27:26).
3. Paul would eventually end up in Rome to witness to Caesar (27:24).

All three predictions came to pass and Paul ended his ministry in Rome (Acts 28). With the Word of God and the influence of the Holy Spirit within each believer, we can receive spiritual downloads and know things to come by revelation of the Spirit. However, God can and does send angels in dreams and visions to at times send important messages, always pointing the visionary to Christ and God's will.

CHAPTER FIVE

ANGELS ASSIGNED TO PROTECT CHILDREN

In my childhood home, there was a picture hanging on the wall of two small children crossing a partially broken bridge and a beautiful angel (a motherly figure with a robe and wings) secretly protecting them as they crossed. It was my favorite picture and actually gave me comfort when I saw it, reminding me that God had an angel who was watching over me. This was important since I slept alone in a small room that often became cold (we used a small coal furnace).

Parents often speak of "guardian angels." However, the phrase "guardian" is not found anywhere in the Scripture. Yet if we carefully examine several key Biblical verses and narratives, there are powerful implications that God certainly does employ angelic supervision on behalf of children.

Christ loved children and set aside time in His busy schedule to pray special blessings over them. Parents would present their infants to Christ to lay His hands upon them and bless them (Mark 10:13). Some of His disciples viewed this as a distraction, even rebuking the parents. Christ was displeased and told them not to interfere with this important ministry. He reminded them that the kingdom of heaven is made up of children (Mark 10:14). Christ would lift the children up in His arms, put his hand upon them, and bless them (Mark 10:16).

Christ gave an interesting revelation concerning children in Matthew 18:10: "Take heed that ye despise not one of these little ones; for I say unto you, that in heaven their angels do always behold the face of my Father which is in heaven." Christ was intent on making it clear that adults should be aware of

63

how they treat (or mistreat) a child, warning that it would be better to tie a millstone (a large rock used for grinding grain) around their neck and jump into the sea than to offend a child (Matt. 18:6). Christ then revealed that angels are assigned to children and continually see the face of God in heaven. This verse brings up several interesting points. God's love for children is so intense that a host of angels who are continually before his throne is assigned to them. But for which reasons?

There are several schools of thought. The context of this verse is a warning about harming or offending a child. Are these angels assigned by God to enact punishment in some form against those who are harming children? Or are these angels commissioned by the Lord to go throughout the earth and oversee the protection and direction of children? Christ said "their angels," meaning children have a personal angel who is with them.

One of my favorite passages that speak of angels' protective assignments is penned in Psalms 34:7: "The angel of the LORD encampeth round about them that fear him, and delivereth them." The Hebrew word for "encampeth" actually alludes to a person pitching a tent with the idea of camping out on a piece of property. One good example is with Job, a wealthy man whom Satan targeted. Satan confessed that a special "hedge" surrounded Job, his property, and his family. Both God and Satan could see the invisible hedge that Job couldn't. Once the hedge was removed, Satan was given limited liberty to attack Job's family, finances, and health. The "hedge" was likely a group of angels who restrained any Satanic forces from entering the property of this godly man.

My father, Fred Stone, was one of the greatest intercessors I have ever known. It was common for him to pray for one hour every day, and when he was ministering at night, he would pray for several hours while meditating on the Word. I heard my dad pray a specific prayer over the family, especially his four children, for many years. It went like this: "Father, I ask you to protect my children [he would name each one] and keep them from harm, danger, and disabling accidents."

During my lifetime, I was in several car accidents and came out with no injuries. Years ago, while I was flying in my ministry plane, the right side of our twin-engine failed and we landed without injury. During another close call, I was exploring the top of an extinct volcano at Crater Lake, Oregon, when I suddenly fell and slid down the steep slope, digging my fingers into the hard dirt; yet I made it to the bottom only sore and dusty, without any injury. In each of these situations, prayer was offered before the event unfolded. Dad continually and earnestly prayed for angelic protection to surround me and the family.

Angels Are Given "Charge"

Psalms 91 deals with God protecting His people to ensure they have long, prosperous lives, and some Jewish Talmudists believe it was written by Moses in the wilderness after the plague of the fiery serpents, after which Israel was more humble and submissive to God.

It is a psalm of protection from danger and in times of war, as noted with these words: "He [God] shall deliver you from the snare of the fowler, and from the noisome pestilence... His truth shall be your shield and buckler...you will not be afraid of the terror by night nor the arrow that flies in the day. A thousand shall fall by your side and ten thousand by your right hand, but it will not come near to you" (Ps. 91:3–7). Verses 11–12 are also interesting: "For He shall give His angels charge over you, to keep you in all your ways. In their hands they shall bear you up, lest you dash your foot against a stone" (NKJV).

The word "charge" here in Hebrew is *sha'al* and refers to placing a demand on someone to do something. In the New Testament when Paul "charged" Timothy, it suggests the military term for when a higher-ranking officer gives a command to a lower-ranking officer (1 Tim. 1:18). In this psalm, God is speaking as the commander, overseeing all of His angelic hosts and placing a military-type instruction for the angels to protect His people. The Hebrew word for "keep" in psalm 91 is *shamar,* and is the same word used in the daily blessing of the High Priest spoken over Israel, which reads, "The Lord bless and keep you..." (Num. 6:24). This word means to "hedge in; to guard and to protect." It is a powerful promise indicating that God directly appoints angels to guard and hedge in His people. Notice the angel is to "bear you up." This Hebrew word for "bear" is *nasa',* meaning to "lift up," and carries a variety of applications in Hebrew throughout the Old Testament. In many instances, it literally or figuratively refers to carrying something, including a person bearing their own iniquities (Lev. 20:19–20). The implication is that angels would *lift a person up* to prevent them from falling into harm.

It should be noted that the sentence does not say "in their

wings they will bear you up," but "in their hands." The Hebrew word for "hands" is *kaph*, and refers to the hollow of the hand. The eleventh letter of the Hebrew alphabet is *kaf*, or *khaf*, and the symbol representing this letter is the palm of the hand. In Scripture, some angels are identified as having wings and others hands, and some both, as indicated when Ezekiel described the cherubim whose hands were under their wings: "And they had the hands of a man under their wings on their four sides; and they four had their faces and their wings" (Ezek. 1:8).

Isaiah describes the seraphim, a unique worshipping angel, as having six wings (Isa. 6:1–2), two of which are used for flying. Zechariah saw a vision of two angels with wings like storks (Zech. 5:9) that were used to carry various items; in this case, a woman in a lead basket. Solomon also penned an unusual proverb in Ecclesiastes 10:20: "Curse not the king, no not in thy thought; and curse not the rich in thy bedchamber: for a bird of the air shall carry the voice, and that which hath wings shall tell the matter."

Some suggest the "bird" here would be a carrier pigeon, as they were used to send messages from the private rooms of the kings and wealthy individuals to faraway locations. However, there may be another application, concealed in this verse. That which "hath wings" in the natural realm would be the fowl or birds of the air. In the spirit realm, however, angels can listen in on secret conversations and report the information to other angels. This is what transpired when the Syrian king secretly planned an invasion of Israel, and twice Elisha the prophet warned the king of Israel to move his troops, in attempts to prevent the ambush. When the king of Syria demanded to know who in his army was secretly spying for Israel, a soldier spoke up, saying, "None, my lord, O king; but Elisha, the prophet who is in Israel, tells the king of Israel the words that you speak in your bedroom" (2 Kings 6:2 NKJV).

This secret military attack spoken of in the Syrian king's bed-chamber was made known by the Lord to Elisha, who was living in Israel. Angels were certainly involved in this scenario, as proven when the Syrian king led his army to Dothan to capture Elisha. Unknown by the king, God had sent angelic horses and chariots of fire to surround the city and protect Elisha from any harm (2 Kings 6:14–16).

The Scripture is replete with verses and narratives indicating God's willingness to commission angels to protect his people from harm and danger. Some Christians prefer not to use the term "guardian angel," as the phrase is missing from Scripture. However, the phrase is an accurate term to identify the assignment of any angel, "given charge to bear up" a child of God.

Applying Protective Principles

Throughout the Old Testament there are what theologians call "types and shadows." A type (from the Greek word *typos*) is an event, person, or narrative in the history of Israel that is a preview of the redemptive work of Christ in the New Testament. The Old Testament is the shadow, but the reality is Christ. For example, the lamb offered at Passover is a "type" of Christ—the Lamb of God who was crucified at the time of Passover.

There are in the Old Testament numerous spiritual principles that have an application under the New Covenant. For example, the High Priest daily blessed the people with a specific prayer of favor and blessing. Christ taught his disciples to pray and ask God for his daily provision. In the tabernacle and Temple, in the morning and the evening, a lamb was offered each day. Thus blood was applied twice daily. The blood of Christ is applied by the confession of our mouth as we "overcome Satan by the blood of the lamb and by the word of our testimony" (Rev. 12:11). Just as the sacrifices were made at the beginning and ending of each day, I have taught the principle that parents should pray a protective hedge over their children in the morning before they walk out of their home and in the evening before they go to bed. This hedge is formed by confessing the blood of Christ over their bodies, souls, and spirits.

In what we call the Lord's Prayer, Christ said we should pray that God would "deliver us from evil" (Matt. 6:13). In Greek, this can read as "deliver us from the wicked one." Satan is called "the wicked (evil) one." It is noted that the phrase "deliver us" has been translated by older scholars to mean "break our chains," or the strongholds Satan exercises over us, as deliverance from Satan requires breaking the yokes and bondages (Isa. 10:27).

Protection comes through the promises of God's word that He is with us always, and will never leave us or forsake us (Heb. 13:5), and that His angels will encamp around us and deliver us (Ps. 34:7). Our part is to verbally confess God's Word out loud and to pray for hedges of protection using the name of Christ and to apply by faith his protective blood. If the blood of earthly lambs could prevent the death angel from entering the Hebrew homes during the Exodus, then the word of our testimony and faith in the blood of Christ can form protective hedges.

We should also pray to the Heavenly Father, petitioning Him to commission His angels to be given charge of all of our bloodline, including infants and children.

CHAPTER SIX

ENCOUNTERING THE DEATH ANGEL

There is a fascination some individuals have with death; not in the sense of experiencing it themselves, but a curiosity with what occurs when a person passes from this life. Their questions include: Is there a soul and spirit within the body? Is there an afterlife? If so, then how are the soul and spirit transported from the earthly realm to the eternal dimension where time is meaningless and the spirits of righteous men and woman dwell (Heb. 12:23)?

From a purely rational perspective, human reasoning has difficulty comprehending angelic-spirit transportation that could thrust a person through a universe of stars and nebulas faster than the speed of light, which is 186,000 miles per second. Longer cosmic distances are measured in "light-years," a term identifying the distance light travels in a year, which scientists have calculated to be 6 trillion miles. For example, the nearest star to us other than our sun is Alpha Centauri, which is 4.37 light-years away. In 1989, the *Galileo* spacecraft was launched from Earth, and it took slightly over six years to reach the planet Jupiter. When the craft entered Jupiter's atmosphere, it was traveling at the fast speed of 106,000 miles per hour! Herein lies the mystery of astronomical travel from earth to heaven. How can the soul and spirit of a departed family member make its way from Earth to the upper celestial world within seconds instead of millions of years?

First, we must comprehend the distance to "heaven," the dwelling place of God. We cannot see His throne using the highest-powered telescope or the Hubble Space Telescope, which has already sent pictures of amazing cosmic signs to Earth. The *Hubble* has peered into distances more than 13.4 billion light-years from Earth, and yet has not found the end of the galaxy or the edge of the universe. This is because there are three noted levels of heaven revealed in the Scripture. When Paul was stoned in Lystra, he had either a vision or an out-of-body experience in which he entered the heavenly paradise, the abode of righteous souls whose bodies are dust of the earth, but whose spirits were transported to a beautiful garden in heaven, to await the resurrection of the dead. Paul said:

> I know a man in Christ who fourteen years ago—whether in the body I do not know, or whether out of the body I do not know, God knows—such a one was caught up to the third heaven. And I know such a man—whether in the body or out of the body I do not know, God knows—how he was caught up into Paradise and heard inexpressible words, which it is not lawful for a man to utter. (1 Corinthians 12:2–4 NKJV)

Paul revealed that paradise was located in the "third" heaven. Biblical research indicates that heavenly space is divided into three dimensions, one layer sitting above the other. The first heaven is the level of Man's dominion, which consists of the air we breathe, the clouds that create rain, and the wind that blows. This is the heaven of the birds and what we call the "sky." The Concorde jet was certified to fly 60,000 feet in the air, and most commercial airlines reach 45,000 feet when transporting their passengers for long distances. This is the level of the first heaven.

The second heaven surrounds the earth in all directions and is identified with the darkness that begins once a craft leaves the earth's atmosphere. The earth's sky is blue during the day as the sun's light hits the earth's molecules and scatters them. When the sun is not shining at night, the sky above is dark. However, in space, the stars are billions of light-years away and space in all directions appears like black velvet with silver dots painted on it. The area of the sun, moon, and stars is called "heaven" in the Bible. The word "heaven" in Hebrew is *shamayim*, and includes both the level where the clouds produce water (*mayim*) and the celestial level of the sun, moon, and stars. This second region is immeasurable and it is impossible to find the edge of the galaxy, at least in this time. Scholars believe that this section of the upper world is where the spirit rebels Paul alluded to in Ephesians 6:12 exercise their dominion.

Our interest is the third level, or the third heaven. This is the highest level mentioned in the Scriptures, although there are extra-Biblical writings (such as the book of Enoch) that attempt to identify seven divisions of heaven, each with a specific characteristic. The idea may have stemmed from the early knowledge that there were seven planets spotted in the sky (including the sun and moon) and each had its own sphere or rule. The books of 1 and 3 Enoch have strange details of the cosmos that incorporate the belief that the second heaven is the dominion of fallen angels and satanic evil spirits, and the third heaven is the paradise of God. Without delving into a noncanonical book, the inspired apostle Paul relates that paradise (the abode of righteous souls) is in the third heaven.

The Angel of Death

This brings us to the angel of death. In the medical field, a person is pronounced dead when the heart no longer beats and brain activity stops. Death in Scripture, however, is much more than the ceasing of bodily functions. Death is a separation of the eternal from the mortal, of the never-ending soul and spirit from the corruptible flesh of a person. The spirit must depart from the body and travel to its eternal destination before the person on earth is dead.

The phrase "death angel," or "angel of death," is not found in the Bible. However, John describes in Revelation 6:8 seeing a horse and rider he identifies as "death and hell." This is not just an apocalyptic symbol or a metaphor, as noted when reading Revelation 20:14: "And death and hell were cast into the lake of fire..." You cannot cast a "symbol" or a "metaphor" into the lake of fire; thus, death and hell are spirits. In the New Testament Greek, the word *hades* is translated as "hell," the abode of unrighteous souls and those who were evil, wicked, or sinners without God's covenant of redemption. Hell is translated as "*hades*" ten times in the New Testament (Matt. 11:23, 16:18; Luke 10:15, 16:23; Acts 2:27, 31; Rev. 1:8, 6:8, 20:13–14). *Hades* can carry three meanings: the chamber of the departed dead under the earth; the chamber of punishment for the unrighteous;

and some suggest it can allude to the grave. Among the ancient Greeks, Hades was a spirit-god that controlled the gates of hell and the underworld.

One of the most intriguing narratives is found in Exodus when God said, "I will pass through the land of Egypt this night and smite the firstborn in the land of Egypt…" (Exod. 12:12). Later we read, "At midnight, the Lord smote all the firstborn in the land of Egypt…" (Exod. 12:29). There was, however, another supernatural being involved the night of the Passover called the destroyer, the spirit that entered the home and took the life of the firstborn child. God instructed Israel to place the blood of the lamb on three spots of the outer doors of their homes, as it would protect their firstborn from death.

Death itself was introduced to man through the sin failure of Adam and Eve. Without access to the Tree of Life, Adam, Eve, and all of their descendants would eventually die. Satan is a literal fallen angel, hell has a spirit controlling it, and death is also a spirit. Death is an "enemy" of God and will be the last enemy destroyed (1 Cor. 15:26).

Death of the Righteous

Christ gave us a powerful true story that reveals what occurs with a righteous and an unrighteous person at the moment of death, recorded in Luke 16:19–31. In the story, a beggar was lying at a rich man's gate, where the dogs were his only friends, licking the sores on his body. The beggar simply asked for crumbs from the table, but the rich man refused to feed this man and ignored his plea. The narrative reveals that both men died near the same time.

The rich man, after he passed with a full stomach "in hell he lifted up his eyes being in torments" and was tortured in the flame (Luke 16:23). When the beggar named Lazarus died starving, we read that he "was carried by the angels into Abraham's bosom" (Luke 16:22). Abraham's bosom is believed to have been a massive subterranean chamber where all of the spirits of righteous saints were assigned, during what we call the Old Testament dispensation, upon their death. When the early patriarchs died, we read that "Abraham gave up the ghost and was gathered to his people" (Gen. 25:8). Many years later, when Isaac died, he "gave up the ghost and was gathered to his people" (Gen. 35:29). When Isaac's son Jacob died, he also "gave up the ghost and was gathered unto his people" (Gen. 49:33). When an infant child dies in the womb (a miscarriage), its tiny spirit departs from its unformed body and returns to God. Job made this clear when he wrote, "Why did I not give up the ghost when I came out of the belly" (Job 3:11), and "Oh that I had given up the ghost and no eye hath seen me" (Job 10:18).

Christ noted that "angels" (plural) and not a single "angel" assisted in the transporting of the soul and spirit of the beggar to his final dwelling place. There have been countless godly men and women who have experienced a near-death or a life-after-death experience. Many describe how men in bright clothes were in the room at the moment they departed. Some were revived and returned to tell their story.

As a young man, my father stood at the bedside of a precious woman of God, a relative who was passing, with several other family members in the room. She was very weak, but still conscious and could speak. Suddenly her eyes opened wide and she turned to the side and said, "Please let the young men in the room." At first, no one paid much attention, then she repeated, "Can't you see them? They are in the corner and they have come for me. Let them through." Within a few moments, she reached out her hand and died. Dad said the young men were angels who had come to remove her spirit from her body and take her to paradise.

My Dad's Departure

Something very unusual occurred just prior to my dad's passing away. He was in the hospital with a blockage that prevented him from eating. After a discussion of adding a feeding tube, he refused and said, "Let me go. I don't want to live this way. I have finished my ministry and it is time for me to go." He was later dismissed from the hospital to a room at Lifecare in Cleveland, Tennessee. For about fifteen days he did not eat or drink. We would take a small sponge, dip it in water, and touch his parched lips. It was a very difficult time for our family, as we watched his frail, physical shell of a body shut down. I spent several days and nights praying, singing a bit, and holding his hand. Memories I will never forget.

Knowing he was passing, I took out my cell phone and captured three pictures of him in the bed, eyes closed and slowly fading. Two of the pictures came out rather dark, but the third one shocked us. There was a strange beam of light coming from the left wall toward his head. I immediately sent the picture to Tommy Bates, who replied, "Oh my... that's the light of the angel of the Lord coming to receive his spirit." Shortly thereafter, Dad left this world for paradise. Much later while looking at the picture, I realized in the days of our healing revival, I had seen a similar photo of a minister taken by a secular photographer. He acknowledged there was no light behind the minister, who stated that when he prayed for the sick, this was the same light (an angel) he would see before great miracles would occur during prayer.

I tried every way possible to create or re-create the light effect in Dad's room and never succeeded. This unique manifestation was a great comfort to the family. When the righteous depart, they are not alone, but the first people they see will be the angels who escort their eternal souls and spirits to paradise.

What You Can "Feel" in a Room

Just as the presence of God can be "felt" and the Holy Spirit shifts an atmosphere during a service, the presence of angels can be felt if a person is in covenant with God and is keen to discern an angelic presence. Several times in my ministry I have sensed the presence of an angel of the Lord, both in private and while I was preparing to minister.

Years ago, during the altar service at a partner's conference at the Smoky Mountain Resort, in Pigeon Forge, Tennessee, I was walking across the platform when suddenly "someone" grabbed the bottom part of my suit jacket from behind. It literally stopped and pulled me, and I felt the bottom of my jacket moving. I thought someone was trying to get my attention, and when I turned, a bit frustrated, to say they should approach me face-to-face, no one was there. However, the man running the soundboard was staring at me like he had seen a ghost. I walked over and said, "Did you see that?"

He said, "I saw you stop and almost fall backwards, and I saw the bottom of your jacket being pulled away from you and no one was there! I almost ran out of the building." I told him it was an angel of the Lord. The man had been drifting away from the Lord, and the incident shook him so much I later heard he began following Christ again.

There is a difference when the Holy Spirit is felt and when an angelic agent is in the room or the sanctuary. The presence of the Holy Spirit moves "out of your belly" (John 7:38), or within your inner spirit, flowing from inside to outside. When the woman from the Bible touched Christ in faith, the Lord said that someone touched Him because he felt "virtue" (literally power) leave his body. When you sense the Spirit of God, it will be inward first. However, the presence of an angel of the Lord is always outward. You have the perception that you are being watched, that someone is in the room and you can't see them, but you know they are there. Angels can be detected through the gift of "discerning of spirits" (1 Cor. 12:7–10). Most charismatics believe this gift is to discern the presence of demons possessing a person. This is part of the operation of the gift, but notice it is "spirits," plural. This gift also enables the receiver to detect the presence of angelic beings.

My father was a pastor for many years, and was many times either at the hospital or the homes of men and women of God when they went to be with the Lord. On one particular occasion, while pastoring in Salem, Virginia, he came home from watching a member of the church pass away at a hospital in Roanoke, Virginia. He said that just before she passed, everyone in the room felt what they described as a strange "electricity in the air," as though the room was "charged with some type of power." This presence arrived a few seconds before the woman died and continued for only a few seconds following. When it came, everyone briefly stopped crying and looked at one another as if to say, "What in the world is happening in this room?" Dad said on many occasions, when the person was a strong believer, the atmosphere would suddenly shift at the moment of death. Although he could not see into the realm of spirits or angels, he would "feel their presence," as their heavenly energy is always outward, or in the atmosphere.

Many believers who have their eyes closed on the brink of death will open them one last time and turn their heads to an empty space in a room, or with a feeble hand point in a certain direction. Those who can speak will begin recognizing family members who passed before them and describe them to be in the room. Doctors say this occurs when the brain releases chemicals that create hallucinations of departed family members. If this were true, then everyone dying should experience similar manifestations, yet they do not. It is also interesting to note that I have never heard one story of a dying unsaved person who saw their loved ones welcoming them. To the contrary, unsaved and unrepentant people, if they are alert, often say they can feel fire moving in their feet and up their legs, and some begin screaming to "get them off of me," and describe strange visions. These manifestations certainly do not occur every time, but there are countless eyewitness accounts where those who were present at the death sensed otherworldly presences in the room.

How Long Does It Take to Arrive in Heaven?

To return to my earlier question, the only immeasurable form of time travel that can theoretically move faster than light would be the "speed of thought." Many ministers believe this may be how angels travel. A spirit being has no physical limitation, and to move through the universe—which is millions of light-years in distance—a faster form of travel is required. An angel or a spirit can "think" themselves from one dimension to another via speed of thought. In this way, distance no longer matters, as the thought process cannot be measured as a length. For example, you cannot measure the distance from heaven to earth.

In the case of Elijah, 2 Kings narrates how the prophet was carried into heaven "alive," riding a chariot of fire pulled by spirit "horses of fire" (2 Kings 2:11). Notice there were no angels with him in the chariot. Angels appear at death, as they are responsible for separating the spirit from the body of the righteous and transporting it to the heavenly paradise. Elijah was not dead or dying; thus the heavenly chariot assisted in some form to move his human body through the cosmos at high and immeasurable speeds, bringing the prophet safely to God's presence, where he will reappear on earth as one of the

two witnesses during the first part of the future great tribulation (Mal. 4:5; Rev. 11:3–6).

God is a spirit (John 4:24), angels are spirits (Heb. 1:7), and
each living human has a body, soul, and spirit (1 Thess. 5:23).
God as a spirit can be omnipresent, or in all places at the same
time. This is not true with angels or humans. Angels in spirit
form move as fast as lightning (Ezek. 1:13–14), and heavenly
beings, when manifesting on earth, often appear in forms of
light or brightness (Ezek. 10:4; Hab. 3:4; Acts 26:13). Angels
can be in only one place at a time, yet they can travel faster
than the speed of light because they are spirits. Each human
in bodily form can be in only one physical location at a time
until the moment they die and their spirit departs from their
body, which can pass through solid objects (John 20:26) and
transport from place to place using the speed of thought. This
is a dimension of movement that men have not yet measured.
You cannot "think yourself" to a place you have never seen or
been. I have never been to Australia; thus, I cannot think of
any location in my imagination and say, "I'd like to go there."

If you had literally stood in the third heaven as Paul did,
then your mind could travel to faraway places you had visited or
seen, and imagine what it would be like to return to that place,
although your body limits the place to where you are. At death,
if you have received Christ as your savior, then angels, being
from paradise, can instantly move from their heavenly location
to earth to release your spirit, which then enables you to time
travel at the same speed as angels.

When Paul was stoned to the point of death in the city of
Lystra, we are never told whether or not he actually died. When

Paul saw the vision of paradise in 2 Corinthians 12, he said, "In the body I cannot tell or out of the body I cannot tell." The phrase "in the body" refers to a vision—a full-color three-dimensional visual image that occurs supernaturally. The term "out of the body" means the spirit is released from the body and travels to a specific location. After the stoning may have actually killed Paul, he may have gone to heaven, and as the saints prayed on earth over his wounded body, his spirit returned to his physical body.

Later in Corinthians, Paul says he "knew a man" (speaking of himself) who had this experience fourteen years prior. This time frame fits with when he was stoned and left for dead, and his alternative account in the city of Lystra (compare Acts 14:19–20 with 2 Cor. 12:2–4). Paul may have actually died, experienced a "life after death" manifestation, and through prayer was raised from the dead. His experience was so sacred to him that, fourteen years later, he felt he could not reveal all that he experienced. Perhaps some of the revelation he later wrote concerning death and the judgment may have been from knowledge he'd gained in this amazing experience.

Angels can "spirit travel" at will since their bodies are of a higher dimension than humans. Once an angel is commissioned to release the eternal spirit of a departed believer to paradise and travel from the earth zone back to the third heaven paradise zone, neither the angel nor the departed spirit is limited by time or space, as angels and the spirits of the righteous dead both have a mysterious molecular structure that enables them to move at incredible speed without harm. Both spirits are invisible to the human eye, but can be seen by all other forms of spirits.

Only when—and if—the veil is removed from the human eyes can they see into the higher dimension of the angelic world, as found in the story of Elisha. He arose one morning and immediately saw horses and chariots of fire surrounding the base of the mountain where he lived, but his servant saw only the Syrian army. That was until Elisha prayed for his servant's eyes to be opened. Suddenly the invisible became visible and the servant, too, saw God's supernatural army of protection (2 Kings 6:14–17). Paul taught that we would all be known as we were known, meaning we will recognize those in heaven if we knew them on earth (1 Cor. 13:12).

Angels at Death: The Release

Hebrews 9:27 explains that, "It is appointed unto men once to die and after this the judgment." In the English translation of the Bible, the word "appointed" is used twenty-three times, as various Greek words with different connotations and meanings. The Greek word for "appointed" in the context of Hebrews 9:27 is different than the other twenty-two references. Here, it means a time in which something has been reserved. We all have reservations about death, should we not go in the rapture of the church. Paul on several occasions thought his death was imminent and even accepted the possibility that he could depart (Acts 21:13). However, it was not God's *set time* or appointed time. I like what Daniel said when he wrote, "For at the time appointed the end shall be" (Dan. 8:19). Your end can only come by a divine appointment, considering Satan no longer carries the keys (authority) of death and hell. Your departure appointment is on God's calendar and not Satan's (Rev. 1:8).

In his final days in Rome, Paul was sentenced to execution. He wrote, "For I am now ready to be offered, and the time of my departure is at hand" (2 Tim. 4:6). A note from my New Testament Commentary on 1 Corinthians 12:1–4 reads that Paul's death was near and he was ready to be "offered." In Philippians 2:17, Paul had spoken of his life's blood being poured out as a drink offering for the cause of Christ. Here, the word "offered" is the Greek word *spendo*, which means to pour out as a libation offering or to devote one's life as a sacrifice. History indicates that Paul was beheaded and his blood poured out. However, he viewed this act as an offering of his life to Christ. The word "departure" in Greek is *analusis*, and alludes to an unloosing of something being woven, such as undoing the stitching in a garment. The departure here was Paul's soul and spirit going to heaven after his death. Paul had written that when he was absent from the body, he would be present with the Lord (2 Cor. 5:8). At death, the soul and spirit are separated from the body; thus we depart this life and enter paradise in the third heaven (2 Cor. 12:1–4).

We must never accept a premature departure. Solomon pondered the question "Why should you die before the time?" (Eccl. 7:17). At times when we know someone is in danger of a premature departure, we should be as the church was in the time when Peter was scheduled for execution. They prayed continually, until the angel of the Lord released him from prison (Acts 12:4–16).

The Dead Saints Are Not Angels

One of the common misconceptions concerning the deceased righteous is that once their human spirit departs its physical body and is escorted by heavenly angels to paradise, they become angels themselves. This unbiblical teaching has caused some to believe that saved people die and become God's angelic hosts, giving them the same unlimited travel potential as God's appointed messengers.

The Bible is clear concerning the deaths of the righteous. All spirits of men, women, and children are transported out of their physical bodies and assigned to "rest" until the resurrection of the dead in Christ at the time of the gathering together of the church. At this present time, any believer who died in covenant with Christ is gathered with the saints of all ages in a special paradise, located in a region called the "third heaven" (2 Cor. 12:1–4). The word "paradise" is used three times in the New Testament: when Christ told the dying thief on the cross, "Today you will be with me in paradise" (Luke 23:43); when Paul wrote that he was in the third heaven and saw paradise (2 Cor. 12:1–4); and when Christ promised the church of Ephesus that if they overcame and entered heaven victorious, they would "eat of the tree of life, which is in the mist of the paradise of God" (Rev. 2:7). The Greek word for "paradise" means a beautiful forest, an orchard, or a beautiful Eden-like garden. The tree of life was originally a heavenly tree transplanted by God to the earthly Eden and designed to keep Adam and his descendants healed and sustaining an endless life. The tree bore twelve different types of fruit each month and the leaves provided healing (Rev. 22:1). After Adam's fall, the tree was guarded by cherubim and flaming swords to prevent men from reentering the garden.

In paradise, the human spirit maintains all five senses that existed in the physical realm and has the same physical appearance that it had while abiding in the body. Since the resurrection of the dead has not yet occurred, there have been departed believers entering the heavenly dwelling for over 1,900 years. They have never aged in their spirit bodies but are not angelic in nature. They will be clothed in their new body at the moment of the resurrection of the dead in Christ.

This fact can also be noted in the Biblical account of the return of Christ, as there will be "saints" and "angels." Paul wrote that Christ would return with "all of his saints" (1 Thess. 3:13), and that when He comes, He would be "glorified in his saints" (2 Thess. 1:10). At Christ's return to earth, the "armies in heaven followed him on white horses, clothed in fine linen clean and white" (Rev. 19:14). These references all allude to the saints, or individual believers who have overcome and are victorious. However, there are other verses dealing with the return of Christ that mention Him coming with "his mighty angels . . . taking vengeance on those who do not know God" (2 Thess. 1:7–8). Christ at His return to set up His kingdom will send His angels with the sound of a trumpet to gather His elect (Matt. 24:31).

Angels are God's eternal beings from the beginning of creation, and the saints are the resurrected believers whose spirits were given a new glorified body at the resurrection of the dead. Christ will bring the spirits of these individuals from paradise to earth when He returns, as Paul wrote, "For if we believe that Jesus died and rose again, even so them also which sleep in Jesus Christ will God bring with him" (1 Thess. 4:14).

Every individual who is in covenant with Christ has nothing to fear at the moment when death arrives. Paul taught that, through Christ's own death, He removed the fear factor and eliminated the "sting" of death (1 Cor. 15:55–56). When a true believer who has repented of their sins and followed Christ takes their final breath, angels will be standing near to release their soul and spirit from their body and escort them to the heavenly paradise (2 Cor. 5:8; 2 Cor. 12:4).

CHAPTER SEVEN

ANGELS WHO ARE CHASING AFTER OUR UNSAVED FAMILY MEMBERS

If you are actively serving Christ and know your name is written in heaven, your greatest burden on earth is to see your unsaved family members repent, turn to Christ, and receive a redemptive covenant of eternal life through Him. For many years I have pondered, outside of prayer, witnessing, and laying claim to a promise of family salvation (Acts 16:31), is there any other spiritual resource we can tap into to assist in reaching our unconverted family members?

It is important to note that, in the New Testament, multitudes were won to Christ after hearing a clear explanation of proving He was the Messiah, either using the Scripture or through a dramatic healing miracle. Today, when a miracle occurs, there is much skepticism—especially in the West—and with various Biblical interpretations, some sinners are more confused as churches argue doctrine instead of presenting Christ as our Savior!

Perhaps there is a source that we should tap into: asking God for angelic assistance in reaching our family. Hebrews 1:14 speaks of angels, and has been taught and interpreted one way, and may have a totally different connotation. If the interpretation I will present is correct, then there is a great promise of how God's attention is turned toward not only saving your lost family members, but assigning angels to assist in the process.

There are several different Bible translations and word studies of Hebrews 1:14:

Are they not all ministering spirits, sent forth to minister for them who shall be heirs of salvation? (KJV)

Are they not all ministering spirits sent forth to minister for those who will inherit salvation? (NKJV)

Are not the angels all ministering spirits (servants) sent out in the service [of God for the assistance] of those who are to inherit salvation? (AMP)

Either Paul or Titus penned the book of Hebrews, or as others believe, a scribe appointed by Paul assisted in dictating the content of this fabulous epistle. It was addressed to the Hebrew (Jewish) believers who had received Christ as their Messiah and were being persecuted for their beliefs. Some out of fear were returning to the rituals at the Temple, which Paul taught were no longer valid to forgive sins (Heb. 6:4–6).

In Hebrews 1, Paul alludes to angels in six of fourteen verses (Heb. 1:4–7, 13–14). His emphasis is that Christ is far better than the angels (Heb. 1:4), and the writer emphasizes that they are spirits (Heb. 1:7). Christians often hear Hebrews 1:14 quoted to indicate that angels are assigned to minister to us as believers, since we are the "heirs of salvation." We are presently "heirs with God and joint heirs with Jesus Christ" (Rom. 8:17). However, in the wording of this verse, the angelic ministry is for those who "shall be heirs," "who will inherit," and "are to inherit."

Paul was formerly Saul of Tarsus, a strict law-observing Pharisee whose mind was set on destroying the new sect that was following the man from Nazareth. Without his knowledge, Saul was marked in his mother's womb by the Lord to be an apostle. He wrote: "But when it pleased God, who separated me from my mother's womb, and called me by His grace..." (Gal. 1:15). In order to reach Saul and break the religious spirit that gripped him, God paid him a supernatural visit on the road to Damascus, where a blinding light came and a voice from heaven spoke to him (Acts 9:3–4). Later in Paul's ministry there were angels connected with his ministry who appeared at times to give him instruction (Acts 27:23).

We know that one of the primary duties of the Holy Spirit is to convict men of sin, then point them to Christ (John 16:8). A sinner cannot be drawn to the Heavenly Father unless the Holy Spirit pulls them. However, it has been my observation, after forty-two years of ministry, that the majority of sinners who turn to Christ are influenced by a person they know—either a family member, a coworker, or a friend they admire and trust.

Many years ago, a noted minister who was traveling throughout the United States had a daughter who was heavily addicted to drugs, and living a wild lifestyle with no interest in following Christ. In fact, at times she would mock her father by pointing out that he was traveling the nation and winning others but was having no impact on her life. Without her knowledge, her father had been intently praying that God would send an angel to visit her and this would cause her to turn her life around. He believed that, for his daughter to be delivered, it required a supernatural manifestation to seize her attention.

One night when the pastor was back home, his daughter came in late, and he heard a scream coming from her room. She ran to him and said, "Dad, he is in my room and scaring me!"

He asked who was in her room and she replied, "It's an angel, Dad, and he's really big! I'm scared!"

Her dad calmly replied, "I'm glad he showed up. I've been

praying for you to see him for a long time!" The encounter did lead to her deliverance from addiction, and she followed the Lord faithfully, until she went home to heaven.

Just as an angel of the Lord connected the Apostle Peter and Cornelius, the Italian Roman centurion—two men that had never met—for the purpose of Gentiles being grafted into the New Covenant, angels can and *do* bring people together, often via a believer who can lead an unbeliever to Christ.

Angels—Connections, Not Conviction

Angels are not assigned to initiate conviction of sin in the heart of a sinner, as this is the responsibility of the Holy Spirit. When a message is preached to the lost, the Holy Spirit activates the need for salvation in the heart of the hearer. The Holy Spirit is always pointing individuals to Christ, as Jesus noted, "He [*the Spirit*] will not speak of himself" (John 16:13), and he will "reprove [*convict to convince*] the world of sin..." (John 16:8; italics mine). An angel's limitation is the inability to be omnipresent—a quality given to the Holy Spirit.

Angels, on the other hand, consistently operate behind the scenes to connect people together for significant purposes. For example, in the past I have experienced a sudden nudge to leave my office and drive through an area without knowing why, only to end up in some restaurant or business. Moments later I would encounter someone who needed encouragement, or was praying for a special blessing. I have walked into stores and felt that the employee behind the counter needed money for a specific purpose. After I handed the strangers money, they confessed they had just prayed for gas money or added income, and the Lord led me their way as an answer to their prayer.

Following the Still Small Voice

Years ago, I flew to Orange County, California, to minister at Free Chapel Worship Center. Before the service began that day, I needed some nourishment. As we discussed a place to eat, just outside the hotel I saw a restaurant and was actually "pulled in my spirit" to the place. I learned years ago not to resist those unusual burdens and strange "nudges" that suddenly press into my spirit at unexpected moments. The place was packed and we waited at the front for a table. Suddenly, through the door walked a well-known NBA basketball star. The woman seating us said, "There is a table near the bar and it's the only one available at this time." Since I do not drink alcohol and am a minister conscious of perceptions, I was hesitant but said, "Okay, I'm in a hurry." Oddly, it was the right place, as moments later, the NBA player came over, pulled up a chair at my table, and we began talking. I knew then that the Lord, through an angel pressing on me and directing my path, had led me to witness to him.

While sitting at the table, I received a word of knowledge that the player's mother's prayers had come up before God and the Lord wanted him to follow Him. He looked stunned, as I knew nothing about him or his mother. He then told me his mom had passed away, and had played the organ at a church for sixty years and she had raised him there. I told him prayers are stored in heaven (Rev. 5:8), the prayer vial of his mother was coming before God, and I was talking to him to confirm that. I proceeded to give him some bad news: that he would lose most of his wealth and he should turn to God, repent, and serve Him. The player grew angry, and he called me a Bible thumper. I continued to give him the Word of the Lord, and when I left, I said, "You may never remember me, but remember what I said. It is coming." Weeks later, the news reported how he had lost most of his wealth, and was headed to a rehab facility to get help.

The Holy Spirit directed me that day, as I am filled with the Spirit and can discern the voice of the Lord. However, why and how did this well-known NBA star choose the same restaurant where I was, at the exact time, and find a table in an area where I would normally never sit? He was unsaved, but because his Christian mother had passed, her prayers were stored in the vials of heaven, and not forgotten. Not only had his mother prayed for him for years, but I later discovered he had a Christian sister who had done the same. I believe the Lord sent an angel to whisper in his ear the idea of going to that specific location at that time, without his knowledge of what was occurring.

It was an angel who gave Cornelius the name of Peter, and told him where he was and what he was to do (Acts 10:1–8). The Holy Spirit can work in the spirit of a believer and give them inspired ideas and thoughts, and direct them accordingly. However, since an unsaved person is not led by the Spirit or listening to the voice of the Lord, an angel's thoughts can be whispered in their ears to direct them in the path of the righteous. From there, the Holy Spirit can take charge.

Chased by an Angel

When David was in great distress, he wrote about the numerous enemies that surrounded him seeking his demise. He asked God, "Let them be as chaff in the wind and let the angel of the Lord chase them" (Ps. 35:5). In this narrative, David needed the Lord to "chase" or "drive away" his enemies, and was asking for divine assistance in this situation. At times, an angel may be needed to prevent a life-threatening accident in the life of someone who is actually not in covenant with God. How can we pray and what can we do when a person we love is away from Christ, without the redemptive covenant, and is in danger?

One of the most dramatic incidents ever to occur in our family was when my father was interceding for his brother Morgan, who had been away from Christ for over forty years. Dad told the story like this:

We were living in North Carolina when the Holy Spirit warned me of an incident involving my brother, Morgan, who had been living in a backslide condition for many years. One afternoon, I was in the parsonage, lying across my son Phillip's bed reading the Bible. Suddenly I heard footsteps to my right side and thought it was my wife, Juanita. Instead the right hand of a man touched me on top of my head. I knew it was an angel, and instantly I had a vision. In it, I was standing about fifty feet in the air above a highway near Iaeger, West Virginia. I saw a terrible accident where a loaded thirty-ton coal truck had rounded a curve and crossed about four feet over the center line, hitting a pickup truck head-on and smashing the entire cab all the way to the truck bed. Inside were the driver and another passenger, who was my brother, Morgan. His head was smashed and hanging in pieces, while arteries spurted blood from his neck. The driver was crushed under the steering wheel.

The Holy Spirit said to me, "This is your brother Morgan. Today he will be killed by a coal truck between the hours of three and four o'clock p.m., unless you pray and intercede." It was already a few minutes before three o'clock, so I jumped off the bed and told Juanita not to allow anybody to disturb me. I rushed next door to the church, where I prayed for the next two hours. The intercession was so stressful; I actually suffered bodily pain while I was praying. I felt like I was wrestling with death itself for Morgan's soul. While I prayed, the Lord spoke to me and said, "Son, I have tried many times through your prayers to reach Morgan, but he won't listen to me. He has willfully turned his back and will not follow me."

I cried out to God, "Why did you tell me to intercede for him? If you cannot reach him, then what am I praying for?"

The Holy Spirit spoke back, "Do you remember years ago when I told you that I would give you two angels, to help you in times of urgent need?" I did remember those angels. While pastoring in northern Virginia, the Lord showed them to me and told me they would not always be with me, but that when I was in urgent need, to call and they would be sent to assist me. "Pray for one of those angels to go and protect Morgan," God said.

Immediately, I pleaded over and over for the Lord to send an angel to protect Morgan. I prayed until I felt a release and the burden was lifted. I went back to the house, exhausted from the experience, and called Morgan. It was about 5:15 p.m. when he answered the phone. Relieved, I said, "Morgan, don't say anything until I tell you what happened." I went into detail about the vision, and the time he would have been killed. I told him God had me intercede to keep him out of hell.

Morgan's voice quivered and finally he was able to speak. He said, "Fred, it happened exactly like you said. We were driving toward Davy, when suddenly I felt a sudden urge to pull over at a small restaurant. I told my buddy, who was driving, 'Pull over at this place. I need to talk to Alan Ball.' We stopped and went inside, but I couldn't remember why I was there. My mind went completely blank. I said to my driver, 'I must be losing my mind. I can't remember why I wanted to see Alan. Come on, let's go.'

"We got back into the pickup truck and continued down the highway. After three or four minutes, we rounded a curve where my neighbor and his wife, who had been driving right behind us, had been crushed to death by a coal truck. You described the scene of the accident exactly the way it happened!"

Several important points should be emphasized in this story. First, Morgan was living a sinful lifestyle away from God for almost forty years, without a redemptive covenant, so he had no supernatural protection in times of danger or threat of death. Second, Dad *was* in covenant with Christ, and because of his intimate relationship with God, he prayed for angels to help Morgan. A similar situation occurred when God was set to scorch the wicked city of Sodom off the face of the earth. Because Abraham had a covenant with God and was Lot's uncle, the Lord sent two angels to Sodom to assist in Lot's rescue. An entire population was eradicated; however, Lot escaped because the Lord sent two angels (see Gen. 19) to rescue him from destruction. This wasn't because of Lot's relationship with Him but because of Abraham's covenant. Without Abraham's intervention, the entire population, including Lot and his daughters, would have perished.

When my son was horribly addicted to drugs and alcohol for about nine years, my wife, Pam, and I prayed continually that the powers of darkness would have "no power to take his life." I based my prayer on Satan attacking Job and assaulting his body with painful sores, but then God said to Satan, "You cannot take his life" (Job 2:6). God limited the influence of the attack to temporary physical pain only, and did not allow Job to encounter a premature death. Because of my son's rebellious actions, some suggested I "remove him from the house." I refused, as I knew that the "serpents" and the "wolves" (wicked people) would attempt to devour him, capitalizing on his addiction.

I replied, "As long as he is in my house, he is under my hedge, and the protective angel assigned in our family lineage will protect him because we are in covenant with God." I spent many hours during those nine years asking the angel to extend God's mercy, despite my son's dangerous actions. I recalled what God said to Noah after the Flood: "For the imagination of a man's heart is evil from his youth" (Gen. 8:21). There were two occasions in which death stalked my son and in both instances the angel of the Lord won the battle. This miracle was not just because of *our* prayers, but the combined prayers of many friends and ministry partners. I boldly asked the angel of the Lord to keep the hedge of protection around my son for the sake of the covenant and for his future purpose.

Note that when an angel came to my dad and *touched* him, immediately Dad experienced an open vision about his brother Morgan's possible accident. The same pattern is in the book of Daniel: When the angel "touched" Daniel, suddenly he received needed strength and hidden knowledge. We read what occurred when the angel came: "I was in a deep sleep on my face toward the ground: but he touched me, and set me upright" (Dan. 8:18). During another angelic visitation, Gabriel, "being caused to fly swiftly, touched me about the time of the evening oblation, and he informed me, and talked with me…" (Dan. 9:21–22).

Angels Manifest in the Midst of Persecution

Kelvin McDaniel is a minister we have supported in the area of missions and worldwide outreach. He has ministered on several occasions in Indonesia, the world's largest Muslim majority nation. Years ago on a Sunday, Kelvin preached outdoors in a village full of radicalized Muslims, using a PA system. He preached only that night, but returned two weeks later.

The pastor of a church there met Kelvin and told him that when he had preached, the people did not like it, and the next morning, two very angry men came in a truck with barrels in the back and began pouring gasoline onto the ground of the church. The pastor said, "My wife and I knelt down in the mud and gasoline, and she cried out to God to prevent them from burning the church down. Several church members living close by gathered and also began crying out to God."

The pastor then said that at that moment, one of the men tried to light a match, but it wouldn't catch. He continued many times with no success. As the people prayed, the pastor tried to talk the man into not burning down the church. Suddenly, the man looked up, shrieked loudly, turned suddenly, and ran away screaming. Two young church members chased him, tackled him, and held him to the ground as he screamed, "Don't let him kill me! Don't let him kill me!"

The pastor told Kelvin, "I couldn't figure out what he was talking about. The man looked like he was fighting for his life. I yelled and said, 'No one is going to kill you,' but the man kept screaming, 'He's going to kill me! He's going to kill me!' I asked him, 'Who is going to kill you?' And he said, 'The angel!'"

The pastor later learned that when the man tried unsuccessfully to light the last match, he looked up at the church and an angel appeared to him. This angel called his name and said, "I am the angel of the Most High God, the one living God, the God of the Bible that this man is preaching. This is God's property and you are trying to burn down holy land. Your life is in danger for being here. Because your heart is not fixed on God, you will die this night if you touch this property."

This man was running for his life. As he was lying on the ground, he began repenting and saying, "I believe. I believe!" About thirty minutes passed before the man was able to get up from the ground. The pastor told him about Christ and the man gave his heart to the Lord.

Kelvin was scheduled to leave Indonesia the following morning. After arriving at the airport, his Indonesian driver received a phone call from the pastor in the village, who asked for him. After taking the phone, the pastor said, "McDaniel! McDaniel! I want you to hear something before you leave. Can you hear this?"

Kelvin said, "I can hear you," and the pastor said, "No not me, the man!"

At first, Kelvin could not hear anything, as the sound seemed far away. Then the pastor said, "That's the man who tried to burn the church down and he was converted last night! He is preaching to people from the roof of his house, and people are stopping to hear what he's saying because it's such an unusual sight!"

If there are family members uninterested in the Word of God, drifting far away from God's presence, or you have children in rebellion, then ask the Lord for an angel to "chase" them and connect them with the right people. This is not a prayer you pray one time then move on. This type of petition must be prayed consistently with faith until you sense a freedom in your spirit that the Lord has heard you.

CHAPTER EIGHT

WHEN ANGELS APPEAR IN HUMAN FORM

Long before social media, cell phone pictures, and advanced recording technology, most stories outside of news agencies were repeated by word of mouth. After being passed from person to person, the original content becomes so embellished at times that the event is unrecognizable to the person who first reported it. Some of the early stories and rumors from the late 1970s and early 1980s told of a male hitchhiker who was picked up by Christians. As they drove together, the unnamed man would announce, "Jesus is coming soon," and suddenly disappear from the car. I heard this story repeated through the years and the location where the man was hitchhiking continually changed. After numerous attempts to trace down the story's origin, I finally gave up. However, the New Testament tells us that two men (angels) did announce Christ was coming again (Acts 1).

While I am uncertain of the accuracy of this hitchhiker story, the fact remains that the Bible teaches that angels can at times take on the form of humans. One verse is Hebrews 13:2: "Do not forget to entertain strangers, for by so doing some have unwittingly entertained angels" (NKJV). The Old Testament records numerous examples of how "men" that spoke, ate, and performed specific duties were in reality angels sent on unique assignments.

One of the great controversial Biblical mysteries is the story of giant men who once roamed the earth before and after the flood. Og, the king of Bashan, had a bed fourteen feet long and six feet wide, based on the length of a cubit (Deut. 3:11).

Goliath, the Philistine champion David slew, was over nine feet tall (1 Sam. 17:4). Without spending pages poring over Biblical, historical, and early fathers' writings on this subject, one theory is that from the time of Adam to Moses, there was no written record of God's word on earth. Angels were instructed by the Almighty to appear on earth in human form to teach men how to live righteously. According to numerous early church fathers, a small group of angels became enamored of the daughters of men, lusted after them, and through illicit intercourse, certain women birthed a race of giants that once roamed the earth (see Gen. 6:1–4).

It would literally require a huge book to answer numerous questions and quote from ancient historical sources, Jewish historians, early fathers, and Hebrew word studies to explain how this was possible. These angels were sent to teach men, but fell into the same traps as humans. These were the "fallen angels" alluded to in 2 Peter 2:4 and Jude 6, who were eventually removed from the earth and sealed in chains in *Tartarus.* The word for "hell" in 2 Peter 2:4 in Greek is *Tartarus,* the lowest hell where the worst spirits are confined until judgment.

During the first 2,500 years of human history, there were extraordinary angelic manifestations on earth, especially in the Promised Land, where angels appeared in the form of a man. One of the most noted instances was when God sealed the day of judgment against Sodom to destroy the wicked cities, yet was restrained by the fact that Abraham had close family members living in the cursed city. The law of God later confirmed that only from the mouth of two or three witnesses could every word be established (Deut. 19:15; Matt. 18:16). The Lord and two male angels (a total of three) visited Abraham to warn him of God's decision to eradicate the evil that had emerged from the people in Sodom, corrupting surrounding cities.

Angels are normally invisible, unless they appear in a dream or a vision. However, in Scripture—including in the four gospels—they appear visibly to Christ. Satan is also an angel, a fallen cherub that directed a rebellion against God. In the narrative where Satan tempted Christ, we read, "Then the tempter came to him and said to him..." (Luke 4:3). The tempter is "the devil" or Satan (Luke 4:8, 10). The question is: Was this temptation in the form of *mental thoughts* that Satan shot in the form of fiery darts (Eph. 6:16), or did Satan himself *appear visibly* to Christ and speak audibly to him? The narrative implies that the test was personally conducted by Satan face-to-face, and Christ heard the voice of his archenemy, as when the test concluded we read, "the devil departed from him and the angels came and ministered to him" (Luke 4:11).

Twice Daniel saw Gabriel, normally invisible, and this mighty angelic prince stood before him "as the appearance of a man" (Dan. 8:15). In Daniel 9:21, Daniel records another encounter with the same messenger and writes, " 'While I was speaking in prayer, even the man Gabriel, whom I had seen in the vision at the beginning, being caused to fly swiftly, touched me...' " (Dan. 9:21). In both visitations, Gabriel is called out by name, but is called "the man" by Daniel—not because the Bible is describing a human, but because Gabriel appeared in a human form.

Gabriel also appears twice in the New Testament. In the Temple's holy place, the priest Zacharias saw "an angel of the

Lord standing on the right side of the altar of incense" (Luke 10:11). In this instance, Gabriel is not reported to look like a *man* but is identified as an *angel*. This is not to say Gabriel did not possess similar human features, but there was something noticeable that caused the priest to understand that this was a being from another dimension, sent from God. Also notice that because of Zacharias' unbelief, Gabriel had the authority to cause him to go mute during the entire nine months of his wife Elizabeth's pregnancy (Luke 1:19–20).

The second appearance of Gabriel was in Nazareth to a teenage virgin named Mary. As Gabriel approached Mary, he called her "highly favored and blessed among women" (Luke 1:28). This greeting confounded Mary, and she was informed she would bring forth a son, a savior, named Jesus. Her only question was how she, a virgin, would give birth without a man? The angel told her He would be conceived through the power of the Holy Spirit. Mary did not reason, question, or doubt, but said, "Be it unto me according to your word" (Luke 1:38). I am certain she knew this messenger was not earthly, as Gabriel's message was part of the Messianic expectations that were predicted hundreds of years earlier by certain prophets.

When angels ministered to Christ after his temptation and during his agony in Gethsemane, then when they later announced his future return at his ascension, they all appeared in the form of men. At Christ's resurrection, the angel who rolled the stone away from the tomb is described with a countenance as lightning, and clothing as white as snow (Matt. 28:3). The guards were afraid and fell to the ground as dead men (Matt. 28:4). Luke describes an encounter in which two men in shining clothes stood outside the tomb announcing Christ's resurrection to the women (Luke 24:4–5). Forty days later at Christ's ascension, "two men in white apparel said, 'This same Jesus which was taken up from you into heaven will so come in like manner as you have seen him go'" (Acts 1:11).

During Christ's ministry, angels (plural) were present. Just as Christ sent forth his disciples two by two, angels can at times minister in groups of two, especially during significant prophetic seasons or when national destinies are altered. At the tomb and the ascension, the angels were in groups of two. Two angels went to Sodom (Gen. 19); in Babylon, Michael the archangel and Gabriel were traveling from heaven to earth bringing messages or battling strong prince spirits that attempted to disrupt God's plan for Israel and the Jews (see Dan. 10).

Angels Taking on Different Forms

Some angelic spirits take on different forms, to the point that their description is difficult to explain. Such is true with the cherubim alluded to in Ezekiel's visions (see Ezek. 1 and 10). The prophet describes a disk like a wheel full of eyes with a life force energy emanating from its center (Ezek. 1:20). God has, at selective times, allowed angels to take on a form that people can see.

During the season of the Old Testament Judges, when God was dealing with Israel and raising up men and women as deliverers to free the tribes of Israel from their internal and surrounding enemies, angels would be directed with specific encouragement and plans that, when followed, initiated supernatural deliverance from their enemies.

In the book of Judges, an angel appeared to rebuke Israel for their lack of total obedience (Judg. 2:1–4). An angel was involved in defeating the king of Canaan and made it known while praising Jael, a woman who took it upon herself to slay an enemy king (Judg. 5:23–24). Gideon was called into battle through the advice of an angel of the Lord who performed signs and wonders before Gideon to confirm he was going to defeat an invading Medianite army (Judg. 6:11–22). God released an angel of revelation to the mother of Samson, giving her instructions that her son would be a Nazarene and deliver Israel (Judg. 13). This angel also gave special signs to confirm the words he had spoken (Judg. 13:20). Once the message was given and heard by the future parents, we read, "But the angel of the Lord did not more appear to Manoah and to his wife. Then Manoah knew that he was an angel of the Lord" (Judg. 13:21). All these angels appeared as men and some were thought to be men, until they performed a miracle of an amazing feat and would suddenly disappear.

An Angel and a Little Girl

At age eighteen, one of my spiritual mentors I gleaned from was Pastor Jim Angle from Blacksburg, Virginia. I remember an amazing story he told me that I believe will inspire you.

Many years ago, there was a doctor named S. W. Mitchell. In the dead of winter with a foot of snow on the ground, Dr.

Mitchell was seated in his house by the fire. There was a knock on his door, and when he answered, there stood a beautiful little blond-haired girl of about six or seven years old, dressed in a red coat, a green hat, white mittens, and white boots. The doctor said, "Come on in, young lady, come in! What can I do for you?"

The little girl replied, "Doctor, I want you to come look at my mommy; she is sick and will die in the next few days if she doesn't get help."

The doctor looked out his window and back at the young girl, and replied, "Well, I'll tell you what. I usually don't do this, but for a little girl to brave this weather like you have, I'll be glad to go and see your mommy!"

The doctor got his bag, and together, he and the girl trudged through the cold, deep snow until they arrived at her house. The doctor followed her through the door and she said, "In there, Mommy is in the room over there," pointing to a bedroom. She continued, "You go in, and I'll wait out here." The door was closed so the doctor knocked on the door, entering the room. He found the mother sickly, pale, and in serious condition. After discovering she had pneumonia, the doctor told her, "Ma'am, if I hadn't gotten here when I did, you would have probably died within two or three days."

The woman weakly asked, "How did you know I was here?"

The doctor answered, "Oh, let me commend you. You've raised your daughter as no other little girl!"

The woman asked, "What daughter?"

The doctor said, "The one standing outside in the living rom."

"Bring her to me," the mother said.

The doctor searched the entire house and there was no little girl. He went back inside puzzled and said, "She was here."

The mother asked, "What was she wearing?" The doctor described the red coat, green hat, white mittens, and boots. The mother began to sob and cry. She said, "You described the outfit of my little seven-year-old who was killed by a car two months ago." She pointed to a closet and said, "If you look in there, you will see the outfit hanging up."

The doctor walked to the closet slowly, and opened the door. There hanging, as though untouched for months, was the red coat, green hat, and white mittens. On the floor were the little white boots.

With the written Word of God and the dynamic power and authority delegated to believers through the Holy Spirit, there may not be the need for angelic appearances in the form of men as there was prior to the church age. However, the invisible side of the angelic world is very much active and continues to do the work of the kingdom, especially as stated earlier, during prophetic seasons.

CHAPTER NINE

RELEASING THE ANGELS OF BLESSINGS FOR HOME AND MARRIAGE

There are four facts about God. First, God is the source of blessings. He said to Abraham, "In blessing I will bless you" (Gen. 22:17). Second, God is a rewarder of those who will diligently seek Him (Heb. 11:6). Third, once God begins to bless you, he will continually add blessings when He observes you are putting His kingdom first (Matt. 6:33). Fourth, God never subtracts from His blessings, but through life, they increase more and more and can be passed down to your children (Ps. 115:14).

The theme of God being the author and supplier of blessings is evident in the numerous times the different forms of the word "bless" are used in the Bible. In the 1611 King James Version, the word "bless" is used 127 times; "blessed" is found 302 times; and "blessing" occurs 67 times, for a total of 496 times the word "bless" is found in some form.

When we speak of blessings, we often think only of people being blessed. However, in the Scripture, many different things can come under the influence of God's blessings. A woman who is barren can become fruitful with children (Gen. 17:6; Ps. 113:9). Children are blessed by the Lord through His Spirit (Isa. 44:3). The homes of those who support ministry are blessed (Ezek. 44:30). God promised to bless the animals on a farm of those who follow Him (Deut. 7:13). Those who practice the giving of tithes and offerings are targeted for God's blessings (Mal. 3:10). The works of our hands are blessed (Deut. 15:10). The psalmist wrote that the Lord would bless His people out of Zion (Ps. 128:5) and bless those who would bless Israel (Gen.12:3).

Angels of Blessing

Angels are not just messengers to announce prophetic events, or bring warnings, judgment, or encouragement to a person. From specific verses in Scripture, angels are also in a position to release specific blessings upon those who follow the Lord. This blessing angel is first alluded to when Jacob, as an old man, is recognizing God's assistance throughout his life and requesting that the Lord will commission the same angel to go with his grandsons, back to the Promised Land: "The Angel which redeemed me from all evil, bless the lads; and let my name be named on them, and the name of my fathers Abraham and Isaac; and let them grow into a multitude in the midst of the earth" (Gen. 48:16).

The Hebrew word for "redeemed" in this verse is *ga'al* and was used in early history to mark a family member or next of kin who purchased back property that was lost through a death, or had to be sold in the event of a financial crisis. In the story of Ruth, Boaz served as her *ga'al* when he stepped forward and said he would redeem Naomi's legal right to have the land of her dead husband restored to her.

When reading the stories of Jacob, there was a specific angel who was with him, even in the times when he was a trickster and deceiver, which got him in trouble with his brother, Esau. This "angel" was also assigned to Jacob's grandfather, Abraham. When Abraham sent his servant to Syria to take a wife from among his people, Abraham comforted his servant saying that, "He [God] shall send His angel before you..." (Gen. 24:7). The servant was concerned the woman would not follow him back to Canaan to marry Isaac (Gen. 24:39). Abraham again reiterated, "The LORD, before whom I walk, will send His angel with you and prosper your way; and you shall take a wife for my son from my family and from my father's house" (Gen. 24:40–44 NKJV).

This was an angel of blessing and favor that moved upon the heart of Abraham's family, and in the process, Rebekah was selected to be Isaac's wife. She took the long journey on camels to meet a husband she had never seen. Now that was a step of faith!

Angels and Your Marriage

Early cultures, and even some today, had prearranged marriages in which the parents selected the companion for their son or daughter. In most Christian cultures, however, the parents pray for God's will and for the "right person" to enter the life of their child at the right time and place. If the child is a strong believer, they, too, are praying for God's perfect will to be done as they mature and meet people who, in the future, could be their potential lifelong mate.

In the beginning when God saw that man was alone, He created for him a helper named Eve. Thus it was the Lord Himself who formed and created the first woman and presented her to Adam (Gen. 2:21–25). As alluded to, when Abraham was concerned about the right woman for his son (as Isaac was in his late thirties and not married), Abraham depended upon the same angel who had led him into the Promised Land to go before his servant and choose the perfect match for his son. When the servant arrived at the exact location and met Rebekah, he explained to her father her assignment, and also made it clear that God had sent his angel to prosper him in what he did (Gen. 24:40). The servant asked for a strange sign that would confirm to him that the Lord had selected the right virgin girl. Abraham's servant had ten camels that needed food and water, and if the woman at the well would care for the camels, she would be the perfect girl for Isaac. All that was in his heart she performed (Gen. 24:42–46). This was truly a "marriage made in heaven," as Isaac was the son of promise, and his future wife would be responsible for two sons, one named Jacob, who would then have twelve sons and initiate the birth of Israel.

When Mary conceived the seed of God's Word, Christ, Joseph was an honorable and righteous man who was preparing to give her a bill of divorcement, since he was not the father. It was the message of an angel in a dream that interrupted the plans of Joseph and instructed him to take Mary as his wife (Matt. 1:20). Joseph followed the instruction, as it is written, "Then Joseph being raised from his sleep did as the angel of the Lord had bidden him, and took unto him his wife" (Matt. 1:24). If Joseph had failed in this mission, Mary would still have birthed Christ but the circumstances surrounding his birth would have always been questioned, especially if she did not have a husband. There were laws in the Torah that Moses wrote that stated a child born through fornication or adultery could not enter the congregation of the Lord to the tenth generation (Deut. 23:2). Joseph should be admired and thanked for his willingness to listen to the angelic dream.

A Word on Whom to Marry

I, for one, am grateful for the Lord speaking in dreams and visions and making the unknown parts of His will for us clearer. As a teenage minister, I had no idea the plans God would have for me and how He would thrust me into an international ministry, reaching over 200 nations and provinces through a weekly telecast. Neither did I see the Voice of Evangelism (VOE) Global Outreach, the Omega Center International (OCI), and Youth Gatherings with thousands in attendance, not to mention overseeing the International School of the Word Internet Bible School. Directing these three major ministries along with working with fifty-five staff personnel and over 200 dedicated volunteers would require a very special companion for me. As a teen, I wanted a pretty wife who could sing and cook well. God, however, saw what I would need long-term and not short-term: someone behind the scenes to handle the cares of life and ministry—a woman who could homeschool my children and care for the small details that are often the "little fixes" distracting my time.

God knew I would need to spend tens of thousands of hours in study and prayer and tens of thousands of hours preparing resource material, taping programs, and writing articles and books. The Lord Himself had to find my wife and I would like to think he sent His angel to "set me up" at the right place and the right time.

I was engaged to be married in June 1981. However, in February, I broke off the engagement and was actually not interested in meeting anyone else. That was, until I met a beautiful teenage Southern belle named Pam Taylor. She was so sweet, a great cook, very quiet, and a bit timid. I fell in love with her almost immediately and during a four-week revival in her home church, the Holy Spirit quickened me that I would marry her. The process that brought me to this point of decision included a series of spiritual dreams that I had several months before beginning the revival. In these dreams I saw her home church (having never been to the church or the town) and I saw the youth group that Pam was a part of.

God is greatly interested in your personal life and your future destiny along with your children, those born and yet unborn. The greatest decision you will make outside of following Christ will be whom you choose to spend your life with—discovering your true soul mate, the one person that can exchange hearts with you.

If you are unmarried and desire a godly companion, there is nothing wrong or selfish with being inspired by the story of Abraham and asking God to send His angel to bring you the right person. It does not mean an angel is going to find you an angel, because men and woman are human with unique feelings and emotions. However, to marry in God's perfect will is the greatest feeling of joy imaginable.

A Generational Blessing Angel

A special angel was assigned to follow the men and their families who would form the nation of Israel. After Abraham was instructed to leave Ur of Chaldea and settle in Canaan land, which would later become Israel, he alluded to the angel when he was preparing to see the second generation of his descendants birthed though his son Isaac. Isaac's son, Jacob, became the heir of the blessing and experienced a vision of a ladder with angels ascending and descending it (Gen. 28). One gave him instructions on returning to Canaan after twenty years in Syria (Gen. 31), and he then wrestled an angel throughout the night (Gen. 32). It is likely that this was the same angel: the angel of blessing that God entrusted to follow each generation of the family to protect, direct, and instruct them.

Jacob was an older man and his sons were grown and having their own children when he finally met Joseph in Egypt. While there, Joseph married and his wife birthed two sons: Manasseh, meaning "God has made me to forget my struggle and toil" (Gen. 41:51), and Ephraim, meaning "the Lord has made me fruitful in the land of my affliction" (Gen. 41:52). Joseph's sons would be adopted into the family, and both of their descendants would be given a land grant, once Israel repossessed the Promised Land under Joshua. Jacob would long be entombed with this people when Israel would depart back home. Yet Jacob prayed and asked the angel to go with his grandsons and make them a multitude in the earth (Gen. 48:16).

This angel was involved in ensuring that Israel's enemies would never destroy them in times of war. At the time of the end, nations of the world will turn on Jerusalem and Israel, requiring God's supernatural intervention. The highest-ranking warring angel will direct this intervention in God's kingdom, Michael the archangel. In the last chapter of the book of Daniel, we read: "And at that time shall Michael stand up, the great prince which standeth for the children of thy people: and there shall be a time of trouble, such as never was since there was a nation even to that same time: and at that time thy people shall be delivered, every one that shall be found written in the book" (Dan. 12:1).

Michael is the main angel whose mission is to stand with Israel and defend her against the final solution of total Jewish annihilation planned by Satan and the Antichrist.

Following the Trail of a Blessing

Jacob was expelled from home and lived as an exile in Syria, with his uncle Laban, his mother's brother, where he worked for twenty years and had his wages changed ten times! Despite hard labor and occasional abuse from his boss (who happened to be his father-in-law), Jacob followed the instructions of the angel and headed back to the Promised Land in great fear, knowing he could eventually encounter his brother, who wanted to kill him last time they were together. However, it is hard—if not impossible—to defeat, destroy, or kill someone with a blessing angel leading their family! As he traveled, we read: "So Jacob went on his way, and the angels of God met him. When Jacob saw them, he said, 'This is God's camp.' And he called the name of that place Mahanaim" (Gen. 32:1–2 NKJV).

The English translation of this verse says, "This is God's *host*." The Hebrew word for "host" here is *machaneh,* and alludes to an encampment of travelers, soldiers, or troops. The Hebrew name *Mahanaim* is a word that means "double camp." This could allude to Jacob's understanding that he was in charge of one large camp of individuals (his large family), and the angels of the Lord formed a second camp to serve as personal body-guards to protect him, as he came near the location of where he saw the vision of angels on a ladder, twenty years prior. Jacob would shortly meet Esau face-to-face, and was uncertain of the reception he would receive. He was very fearful and knew Esau could kill him and his entire family if he chose to. Jacob divided his family between Leah and her children, and Rachel with Joseph in the back of the pack. In case Esau killed Leah and part of the family, his favorite wife, Rachel, could escape!

As part of his restoration with Esau, Jacob prepared a large "gift" to present to his estranged brother: a portion of the animals that Jacob had herded from Laban's farm. He had not stolen these animals—they were a part of his wages paid to him for working for twenty years. Esau's gift included:

- 200 female goats
- 20 male goats
- 200 ewes
- 20 rams
- 30 female camels and their colts
- 40 kine (cows)
- 10 bulls
- 20 female donkeys
- 10 foals

Hundreds of years after Jacob presented this gift to Esau, in the time of the Tabernacle and Temple, offerings presented to the priesthood that were not animal offerings were considered bloodless and voluntary offerings, such as grain and oil. Jacob asked Esau to receive the "present" from him of these numerous animals: "And Jacob said, Nay, I pray thee, if now I have found grace in thy sight, then receive my present at my hand: for therefore I have seen thy face, as though I had seen the face of God, and thou wast pleased with me" (Gen. 33:10).

The Hebrew word here for "present" is *minchah*, the word used occasionally in the Old Testament later for a voluntary offering, as mentioned above. This word is used early in the Torah when Moses wrote about Cain's offering of the fruits that were presented to God (Gen.4:3–5). So why did Jacob give this gift to Esau? The best explanation is that Jacob was fulfilling the vow he had made to God twenty years prior when he said, "If you bring me back again, I will give you the tithe—or the tenth." Yet it appears that Jacob was determined to give away a portion, possibly a tenth, as his offering to God and gave this present to his brother, Esau!

Wrestling for a Blessing

After preparing this offering and before meeting Esau, Jacob suddenly encountered an angel whose words and actions would forever change his life and destiny:

> And Jacob was left alone; and there wrestled a man with him until the breaking of the day. And when he saw that he prevailed not against him, he touched the hollow of his

thigh; and the hollow of Jacob's thigh was out of joint, as he wrestled with him. And he said, Let me go, for the day breaketh. And he said, I will not let thee go, except thou bless me. And he said unto him, What is thy name? And he said, Jacob. And he said, Thy name shall be called no more Jacob, but Israel: for as a prince hast thou power with God and with men, and hast prevailed. (Genesis 32:24–28)

This wonderful encounter occurred one night before Jacob came face-to-face with Esau. This angel of the Lord changed Jacob's name to Israel and touched his thigh, giving him a limp for the rest of his life. Jacob was always on the run and his "limp hip" would slow him down so he could no longer run from men or God!

Note the number of times and places where an angel or a host of angels were a part of his dreams and life:

- Jacob dreamed the dream of the ladder of blessing with the angels of God (Gen. 28:12).
- An angel visited him in Syria telling him to return to the Promised Land (Gen. 31:11–13).
- The angels met him prior to meeting Esau (Gen. 32:1–2).
- Jacob wrestled an angel of the Lord and received a spiritual transformation (Gen. 32:24–25).

The blessing of Jacob was undeniable. He left home with nothing and found a job with his mother's brother in Syria. He worked diligently and eventually left with twelve children and countless animals. In twenty years, God had changed the heart of his brother, Esau, and when they met, Jacob told Esau to take the gift of animals, because he "had enough" (Gen. 33:10–11). Even his father-in-law, Laban, understood the power of the blessing when he said, " 'Please stay if I have found favor in your eyes, for I have learned by experience that the LORD has blessed me for your sake.' Then [Laban] said, 'Name me your wages, and I will give it' " (Gen. 30:27–28 NKJV).

Jacob then confessed to Laban, "For what you had before I came was little, and it has increased to a great amount; the LORD has blessed you since my coming" (Gen. 30:30 NKJV).

In psalm 103:20, it is written: "Bless the Lord, you his angels, who excel in strength, who do his word, heeding to the voice of his word."

Meeting an Angel of Blessing

A most amazing event occurred to my VOE office manager's sister. I have asked her to relay this for you:

> In April of 1999, I was engaged to be married to Jeremy Reid. We had saved money for over a year and found the perfect starter home for Jeremy to live in until our wedding in August. Because the house was in a rural area where there was a volunteer fire department, the department required proof that the local fire dues were paid before we could close on the house. The day before we were to close and pay the fire dues, our broker called and informed us that we needed an additional $400 for closing the next day.

I knew we did not have the money and our parents could not assist because they were paying for the wedding. I stopped and prayed and told the Lord that I knew this was supposed to be our house, and that somehow I would pay those fire dues and He would just have to work it out for me. After arriving at the fire station, they told me that I needed to get a number from a plaque that was posted on a tree in the yard, which they used to identify who paid their dues. I drove to the house and was standing in the front yard looking at the plaque when suddenly a man pulled into the driveway. I was frightened because I was alone and he was a very large man. He exited his car and came straight towards me in one swift movement and said, "The Lord told me to give this to you." He pulled a large amount of cash from his pocket and handed it to me. Before I could respond, he was back in his car and out of the driveway! I immediately headed to my car to follow him. As he went around the curve, it was as though he simply disappeared! I drove around looking for him and found neither him nor the car.

When I finally stopped, I counted the money and was stunned to discover twenty $20 bills. I had not told anyone about needing the additional money, so I joyfully headed to my parents' house to tell my mom about this strange answer to prayer. After going in, I passed a picture of my grandparents on the mantle, which I had passed many times over the years. This time I stopped cold when I looked at the picture and saw who appeared to be the same man who had handed me the money. He looked exactly like my grandfather, who had died before I was born. I never knew him or my grandmother, but the look was identical.

To this day I cannot understand how God did this or who the person was, but to me, it was a messenger of the Lord—perhaps an angel who took on a human appearance and brought me the miracle I needed to meet my needs at that moment!

God is the source of all true blessings, both spiritual and material, and He appoints His heavenly messengers to assist us in discovering His will on earth, linking us up with a life companion and help in providing finances to meet our personal needs. While we may never visibly see an angel of the Lord, angels never require physical rest as they continually oversee God's plans and promises to bless and prosper the righteous.

CHAPTER TEN

ANGELS BATTLING DEMONS IN YOUR HOME

The Shepherd of Hermas is an ancient text from the second century AD. This vision was considered by many of the early church theologians as inspired, and was commonly read in the early church to believers. Without going into too much detail about the vision, the seer, a shepherd, mentions a guardian angel who protects each believer against an opposing agent of the devil, who is assigned to hinder each person. Concerning this thought, the shepherd speaks with an angel. The manuscript reads:

> There are two angels with a man—one of righteousness, and the other of iniquity. And I said to him, "How sir am I to know the powers of these, for both angels dwell with me?" "Hear," he said, "and understand them. The angel of righteousness is gentle and modest, meek and peaceful. When therefore he ascends to your heart, forthwith he talks to you of righteousness, purity, chastity, contentment and every righteous need and glorious virtue. When all of these ascend into your heart, know that the angel of righteousness is with you. These are the deeds of the angel of righteousness..."[1]

A good question has been asked: If there are over 7 billion people on earth, how could everyone have an angel? The answer is "everyone" does not have an angel. If they are in a

1. *The Shepherd of Hermas*, in *Ante-Nicene Fathers*, Vol. 2, p. 266.

false religion, worship idols, not in covenant with God, or are wicked or evil, there is no godly protection assigned over them. Also, angels are not with a person twenty-four hours a day and can move at the speed of thought, and one angel could perform perhaps thousands of assignments in a single day. Angels do not just stand and watch you study, eat dinner, or take a shower in the morning. They minister to specific needs and situations or protect from danger and premature death.

An example is found in Daniel. Angels were present only when he needed to understand a vision, and when he faced death in Babylon in the lions' den, and when his three companions were thrown into the furnace of fire. A "fourth man" was observed in the flames, who was an angel protecting the men from being burned to death (Dan. 3:25).

Saint Athanasius (c. 296–373) was an influential leader who was also known as the "Father of Orthodoxy," or as some Protestants label him, the "Father of the Canon." He wrote: "For there are many Archangels, many thrones, and Authorities, and dominions, thousands of thousands and myriads of myriads, standing before him, ministering and ready to be sent."[2]

Saint Athanasius based the number of angels on a verse in Revelation 5:11: "Then I looked, and I heard the voice of many angels around the throne, the living creatures, and the elders; and the number of them was ten thousand times ten thousand, and thousands of thousands" (NKJV).

Based on the information available in Revelation 5, around

---

2. "Discourse II Against the Arians," in *Nicene and Post-Nicene Fathers*, Chap. XVII, Ser. II, Vol. 1, p. 362.

God's throne there are twenty-four elders (Rev. 5:8) and four living creatures (Rev. 5:14). Many believe the redeemed saints are in heaven singing the chorus John heard, "Worthy is the lamb..." (Rev. 5:12). If these voices, however, are the host of heaven, angels, there are "ten thousand times ten thousand and thousands of thousands." If taken literally, the number here is 100 million. John then adds "and thousands of thousands." In reality, he is stating that the number of the heavenly hosts cannot be measured.

Daniel saw a similar vision of heaven and the angels, and said, "Thousand thousands ministered unto him, and ten thousand times ten thousand stood before him" (Dan. 7:10). Psalms 68:17 expands on this thought by saying, "The chariots of God are twenty thousand, even thousands of angels..." The prophet Micaiah saw a vision with God sitting on his throne, and the host of heaven on his left and right side (2 Chron. 18:18). In the book of Job, the writer describes a heavenly counsel meeting with the "sons of God" (angels) and Satan, the accuser, was mingling among them (Job 1:6–7). The point is clear: There is no shortage of angels to battle demonic assignments and minister to the saints.

Angels become involved in battling the Satanic forces of darkness. In Daniel 10, there were two principal spirits that attempted to exercise dominion over the government leaders of Persia, called the "prince of the kingdom of Persia" (Dan. 10:13), and also a second spirit that would be involved with the future empire of Greece, called "the prince of Grecia" (Dan. 10:20). The angel told Daniel he "remained with the kings of Persia" (Dan. 10:13). The angel further revealed that when he concluded speaking with Daniel, he would return to fight with the prince of Persia, who was the demonic entity ruling over Persia. When the battle concluded and the angel departed back to heaven, then the prince of Greece would come. This historically occurred many years later, when Alexander the Great, the Grecian military general and king, overthrew the kings of Persia, setting up his headquarters in Babylon.

Marking Your Home

The early civilizations were knowledgeable of the existence of a spirit world. In ancient Mesopotamia, people would place symbols and, at times, gods at the entrances of their homes and temples, to prevent the wrong spirits from entering their house. During the Exodus, the lamb's blood was applied to the left, right, and top posts of the outer doors to prevent the angel of death from entering the home and taking the life of the firstborn (Exod. 12). Once the twelve tribes entered the Promised Land, they were to mark the post of their homes with the Word of God (Deut. 6:9). This law eventually led to the creation of a mezuzah, a small object that contains rolled parchments of Scripture that is attached to the right side of the front door of a devout Jewish home.

Evil spirits possess people and their homes. According to Christ, when an unclean spirit departs from a person, either willingly (by its own choice) or by being "cast out" (Mark 6:13), the evil spirit seeks to return with seven other spirits more wicked than himself, entering in and dwelling in the "house" he initially departed from (see Matt. 12:43–45). The Greek word used for "house" in the passage in Matthew is *oikos*, and can literally or figuratively mean "a family." When the adversary controls one family member, they can impact the entire family, or the "house." Spirits are not interested in dwelling in an empty old building, as the television series of *Ghost Hunters* implies. Spirits desire a human body.

When the Hebrew nation of 600,000 men and their families departed from Egypt, God Himself had initiated plagues that were in reality a direct attack upon Egypt's false gods, to prove to the Egyptians that not only was the Hebrew God superior to Egypt's dead deities, but Yahweh was the only true God in existence. The Hebrew tribes were to repossess the land of their fathers Abraham, Isaac, and Jacob, and were forbidden to mingle their religious beliefs with surrounding pagan tribal idols. God forbade the people from any form of idolatry, especially bringing idols into their homes. One reason He did so was because idols attract evil spirits and open an entrance to the home of those who bring recognition or worship to such false objects.

Many believers unknowingly crack open an entryway for demonic activity in their homes by the very things they allow inside. Those who have formally been involved in Satanic or occult activity or in false religions are more aware of this than those raised in church.

Everyone Began Falling

I am a collector of ancient coins and antiquities. Years ago I made a negotiation for a large collection of glass, clay, and metal objects dating back 1,800 to 3,400 years. Most of the items had been in homes or businesses, with the exception of the old daggers and spears, which had been in the possession of soldiers. While these items were being stored in the VOE ministry center, something strange began to occur. My wife, Pam, fell and tore the meniscus in her knee, followed by the OCI director, Tammy James, who fell and tore her ACL. One of my phone workers fell in a restaurant and tore her knee. One of my VOE bookkeepers fell while watching her grandchildren and broke her ankle, requiring months off work to recover. My mother left work for lunch, fell, and broke her ankle and right wrist, and spent ten weeks recovering in bed. We knew this was a physical attack but could not get a revelation as to why or what the source was.

One afternoon while we were working upstairs at VOE, Tammy saw out of the corner of her eye a dark shadow of a man passing across the room, from the area of the swords and spears. She knew it was a spirit and immediately said, "This is connected to those knives and daggers." That is when I remembered the story of the "Spear of Destiny," a spear dating to Roman times that was reportedly used by the centurion at the cross to pierce the side of Christ. It became a "holy relic" and was sought by kings and world leaders, based on a tradition that whoever possessed the spear would rule the world.

This spear bears a strange occult history, including the story that Adolph Hitler, as a young man, spent time at an Austrian museum staring at the spear when he saw a spirit appear behind the glass showcase. Hitler would years later invade Austria and confiscate it, placing it in a Berlin bunker. When kings or world leaders possessed this spear, they dominated militarily, and when it left their possession, they lost power or control. After this shadowy spirit appeared, I removed the spears from the property and no longer possess them.

I am sure some of you are asking, "How could an old iron object attract some spirit?" The answer is found in the link with shedding blood. There is no way of knowing who was slain in battle by these ancient weapons. Evil spirits are attracted to blood, and I believe it was best not to open any more doors that could cause an injurious situation.

When Joshua and Israel conquered Jericho, there was a warning given to the soldiers not to personally take any objects from the city for themselves: "And you, by all means abstain from the accursed things, lest you become accursed when you take of the accursed things, and make the camp of Israel a curse, and trouble it " (Josh. 6:18–19 NKJV). One man in ancient Israel was soon to discover that bringing accursed things into your dwelling place can cost you not only the "victory," but eventually your life!

Jericho was the first of approximately thirty-one Canaanite cities that Joshua and the Hebrew warriors conquered. Jericho was a "first fruits" city. All the spoils gathered during this conquest were to be given to the treasury of the Lord's Tabernacle as a first fruits offering: "But all the silver and gold, and vessels of bronze and iron, are consecrated to the LORD; they shall come into the treasury of the LORD" (Josh. 6:19 NKJV). The first fruits belong to the Lord, and if withheld, not only are they cursed, but all of Israel would be "accursed" (Josh. 6:18–19). The word for "accursed" is *cherem*, and alludes to a doomed object or something marked for destruction. If Jericho's first fruits were withheld, then the objects would become a curse and not a blessing.

During the conquest of Jericho, a man from the tribe of Judah, Achan, secretly seized some gold bars and a beautiful Babylonian garment and hid them in his tent. As a result, when the Hebrew troops engaged in their second military campaign at a small city named Ai, several Israelites were slain and Israel experienced defeat. In frustration, Joshua reminded God that He had not kept His word that Israel would defeat all her enemies (Deut. 11:25). God commanded Joshua to "get up" and listen, and revealed the reason for Israel's defeat. Someone had disobeyed God's instruction and was hiding accursed things among their possessions. Only when the sin of Achan was exposed and the cursed items were removed from Achan's tent was God's blessing restored and Israel defeated her enemies (Josh. 7:24–26, 8:1–2).

The Spirits in the House

At this point I wish to share a personal family incident that will help explain how a demonic "open-door policy" works. Years ago, my son Jonathan became addicted to certain types of drugs and was secretly taking pills and mixing them with alcohol. His room was upstairs, and at times he would be up all hours of the night. On one occasion, we ended up taking him to the emergency room for taking too many pills as his mother and I battled in the spirit realm, requesting that God would be merciful to him during this season of rebellion and Satanic attack designed to prematurely take his life.

One night at about three in the morning, I was jolted awake by my son shaking me, asking me to get up because he needed to talk to me. Pam also awoke, and soon his little sister was out of bed, too. We went into the living room and he said, "I've done some things that have allowed demon spirits in the house." As he began confessing, I knew some type of evil spirit had been given access to his living area, and was mentally tormenting him. Within minutes, my wife marched upstairs, and with a loud voice and great authority, she began demanding that every wicked and unclean spirit be expelled not only from the area where it was controlling Jonathan but from the entire premises, as she reminded every spirit that this was a "house dedicated to God" and "we as the parents were in covenant with God and no demonic power had any legal authority in our house!" Within thirty minutes my son was dragging out three garbage bags full of all sorts of junk he had hidden in the attic and throughout his room. That night was an initial breakthrough, but there was something else we would discover that reveals the dangers of spirits having access to a home.

My Daughter's Attack

When my daughter turned fifteen, she gave her testimony in front of 5,000 young people at our OCI ministry facility that neither her mother nor I knew was coming. She is a very loving, caring, and wonderful girl that had never given us one problem. But she confessed a secret addiction.

That night, she spoke of how she first saw pornography on an iPad when she was eleven, and this led to a three-year on-and-off addiction. She had finally become so tired of the bondage that she cried out to God in her room and He literally delivered her. She then became friends with several spiritually strong young girls in our youth group who love worshipping and praying, and this had helped her in maturing in her faith.

I later put two and two together. Her room was just below her brother's, and at the same time our son was battling similar issues, the spirit he admitted to bringing into the house was also attacking my daughter, who was at that time too young to actually understand what was happening and how to counter it with spiritual authority. I do realize there must be a balance when teaching about demonic activity in the home, as the majority of our home problems are the works of the flesh: a bad attitude, rebellion, anger, and so forth. However, believers must understand that if we begin dabbling with things that attract dark spirits, they will more than take advantage of the situation.

Angelic Reinforcements

Believers know that our spiritual authority over all the powers of the enemy is found in three warfare resources. First is the power of the Word of God. During his temptation, Jesus quoted three Scriptures located in the Torah (from Deuteronomy), to counter Satan's temptation. The Word became a "sword" of the Spirit (Heb. 4:12). The second weapon is the power of the blood of Christ. Christ's blood is the source of redemption and all spiritual blessings. Satan is overcome by the blood of Christ (Rev.

12:11). The third weapon for spiritual warfare is the second half of Revelation 12:11: We "overcome...by the word of our testimony." The word for "testimony" here, in Greek, is *maturia*, and refers to judicial evidence. It is testimony given by a witness in court. These three spiritual resources—the Word, the blood of Christ, and the word of our testimony—are significant as angels are attracted to these spiritual weapons. Just as unclean spirits are attracted to those things related to sin, the flesh, and the spiritually and morally unclean, the presence of the Holy Spirit and the angels of the Lord are attracted to the Word of God, to the worship of God, and to prayer.

Since angels respond to the voice of the Lord and to God's Word, it is important that when confessing and "claiming" a promise we speak God's Word out of our mouth and place it deep within our heart. When Christ was tempted three times, he quoted three passages from Deuteronomy in response to Satan's temptations. Afterward, angels came and ministered to him (Matt. 4:11). Throughout history, angels have battled Satanic forces, and in every instance, the angel came out on top, and they will continue to do so!

CHAPTER ELEVEN

WHEN HEAVENLY WATCHERS MAKE EARTHLY DECREES

This matter is by the decree of the watchers, and the demand by the word of the holy ones: to the intent that the living may know that the most High ruleth in the kingdom of men, and giveth it to whomsoever he will, and setteth up over it the basest of men.

Daniel 4:17

The book of Daniel is considered an apocalyptic book of the Bible. The terms "apocalyptic" and "apocalypse" refer to sacred Biblical literature that uses unusual symbolism to conceal the true meaning of the text. Within the prophetic books of Daniel and Revelation, angels play a significant role in bringing understanding to the symbolism or knowledge of specific dreams or visions given to the prophetic seer.

In the book of Daniel, God sends delivering angels to close the mouths of lions, preserving Daniel from being a late-night meal for the hungry "king of the beasts" (Dan. 6:22). In a second amazing deliverance, a protective angel prevents three Hebrew men from becoming a pile of ashes in a furnace of fire (Dan. 3:28). Angels are also commissioned to bring specific messages to the prophets, including, in Daniel's case, insight into the far future and on the future Antichrist, his ten kings, and the final kingdom formed on earth before Christ returns.

The early and later parts of the book of Daniel were written in Hebrew. However, a large portion was written in Aramaic, as it was a common language spoken throughout the Assyrian and Babylonian Empires. Three times in Daniel, the Aramaic word for "watcher" is used for a guardian angel, in 4:13, 17, and 23. The word in Aramaic is *iyr*, and the other phrase used is "holy one," which in Aramaic is *qaddiysh*. The word alludes to one who "watches, or is awake."

The Watchers in Eden

The first reference to angels assigned to keep a continual "watch" is found immediately after Adam and Eve were expelled from the Garden of Eden. God placed cherubim with a flaming sword to guard the entrance to prevent Adam, Eve, or their future descendants from reentering the garden and eating from the tree of life, thus living forever in a sinful condition (Gen. 3:22–24). These special angels turned in every direction—north, south, west, and east—to prevent any living person from gaining access to the tree of life.

The watcher story in Daniel begins with King Nebuchadnezzar. This famous king of Babylon had constructed the most elaborate city in world history, up to his time. He had led his armies into Judea for personal purposes, to capture the smartest Jewish youth, who were then placed under supervision in the king's court. They were to be taught the Aramaic languages, providing the king with the ability to communicate to the Jewish people, most of whom spoke Hebrew. Nebuchadnezzar had also seized a long list of gold, silver, and bronze treasures, and placed them in his Babylonian treasure houses. (For a list, see Jeremiah 51–52.) The arrogant king burned the temple of Solomon to the ground and left God's holy city in smoking ruins. He followed up by chaining the Jewish captives and leading them on about a four-month walking journey, 900 miles away into Babylon.

Imagine the spiritual, emotional, and physical condition of

the Jewish people, knowing that many would never return to Jerusalem but, because of their age, would die and be buried in this foreign land. The depression was so strong, a psalm tells us that when the Babylonians wanted to hear the Jews sing the "Lord's song," their response was to weep, hang their harps on the willow trees, and say, "How can we sing the Lord's song in a strange land?" (Ps. 137:1–4).

Long ago in Israel's early history, God spoke to Abraham's descendants and revealed that He would bless those that blessed Israel, and He would curse those that cursed Israel (Gen. 27:29). Years after Jerusalem's destruction, Nebuchadnezzar was troubled by a nightmare in which he saw a large tree covered in fruit with birds resting on its branches. He heard a voice telling a "watcher" to cut down the tree but leave the stump in the ground: "I saw in the visions of my head upon my bed, and, behold, a watcher and a holy one came down from heaven; He cried aloud, and said thus, Hew down the tree, and cut off his branches, shake off his leaves, and scatter his fruit: let the beasts get away from under it, and the fowls from his branches: Nevertheless leave the stump of his roots in the earth…" (Dan. 4:13–15).

In the dream, an angel cut down the tree and then passed over the stump seven times. Daniel interpreted the dream as a warning that the king would encounter a mental breakdown and live like a wild beast in the field for *seven years*. Eventually, he would recover and return to power. The entire dream was fulfilled one year later (Dan. 4:28–31), when a voice from heaven announced that Nebuchadnezzar's kingdom was taken from him, and he experienced a complete mental breakdown.

The Decree of the Watchers

The most interesting aspect of this amazing historical narrative is the unseen activity occurring in heaven, as angels planned for Nebuchadnezzar's mental breakdown and his removal from power for seven years. The decision was made by a decree in the heavenly courts twelve months before it was enacted.

Daniel informed the king that this dream would occur if he did not repent, as the warning was sealed by "The decree of the Most-High" (Dan. 4:24). "Decree" is a word of Aramaic origin that refers to a determination that has been made in a *legal matter*. In this case, God had been observing the actions (pride) of Nebuchadnezzar and his treatment of the holy temple, the holy city (Jerusalem), and the holy people, the Jews: "This matter is by the decree of the watchers, and the demand by the word of the holy ones: to the intent that the living may know that the Most High ruleth in the kingdom of men, and giveth it to whomsoever he will, and setteth up over it the basest of men" (Dan. 4:7).

Two types of angels are referred to in this verse: the "watcher" and the "holy ones." By definition, "watchers" are angels with a specific mission, including personal oversight into select people, nations, or situations. The "holy ones" are basically the holy angels in general. Notice the watcher is to ensure that the decree is enacted, as the king's dream indicated that a watcher would cut down the tree, initiating the loss of mental capability within the king. There was a "demand" placed by the holy ones with the intent of making the king and others know that God Himself is in charge of the affairs of men, as it is written, "He rules in the kingdom of men" (Dan. 4:7).

The Aramaic word "demand" here is unique. *She'ela* is more than just a written or verbal demand for something to occur. It carries the idea of a question present in a legal case in which information is gleaned and a judicial demand is made, but made based upon the information presented. Thus, the watching angels, perhaps for years, were observing the actions and words of this Babylonian king, and owing to his actions against the Jews, the holy Temple, and Jerusalem, and his arrogance (Dan. 5:20), he was assigned a decree for a temporary form of judgment, as a punishment for his evil actions.

There is also a possible second interpretation for the phrase "holy ones" that refers to individuals who are set apart for the purposes of God—either a heavenly and an earthly messenger; an angel or a human. In the Torah, the Jewish people are called "a holy nation" (Exod. 19:6). The chamber where God's presence dwells in the tabernacle is the "holy place" (Exod. 3:5). The Sabbath day is called "holy" (Exod. 16:23), and certain garments can be set aside as holy (Exod. 28:2). The sacred anointing oil is also holy (Exod. 30:31). In the rabbinical understanding of the Holiness of God and the ancient temple, something that was less holy could be sanctified and become more holy, but it was sinful for something that was holy to be used in a profane manner. For example, there was a holy fire on the brass altar ignited by the hands of the priests used for burnt offerings, and there was holy incense burnt on the golden altar that was mixed by a specific formula, not to be duplicated. However, on two different occasions, two sons of the high priest offered their own "strange fire" and were struck dead for attempting to fake holiness. On a second occasion, Korah, a rebellious leader, crafted his own incense censors and offered his own before God, which actually "incensed" or angered Him, releasing immediate wrath toward Korah and his team of rebels (Exo. 26; Lev. 10:1–2; Num. 16:1–49).

As for the watchers in Daniel, tens of thousands of Jews were in Babylonian captivity, remembering the shrieks of screaming neighbors and the smell of burning homes colliding with the sounds of clinging metal chains that bound the hands and feet of thousands of Hebrews, dragging their weary bodies across the ancient deserts toward Babylon, a pagan city ruled by a pagan king. It may have been the "demand of the holy ones," or the prayers for God's vengeance rising upward from the lips of the Jewish captives themselves, that reached the heavenly court where the prayer decree was presented to God. The judge of the universe sent His verdict in the form of breaking the pride of Babylon's King Nebuchadnezzar.

Warning to Preachers

The following story involves a personal ministry friend who has since gone on to be with the Lord, after recovering from a spiritual fall and being restored in the later part of his ministry. When he was a young teenager, he was called into ministry and from the outset was an anointed minister. In his twenties, he was preaching at large conventions with thousands in attendance and was noted for seeing great spiritual results in the altars.

Before he hit the age of thirty, he was voted in as pastor of a large, prestigious church, and within months the attendance was overflowing with people coming early for both the morning and the Sunday night services just to find a seat.

It was during the peak of his ministry that a fellow minister from outside the United States experienced a very strange warning vision, and knew he must share it with the minister. In the vision, he saw Jesus standing beside this minister. He was growing tall and great, actually becoming larger than Jesus. It was then he saw an angel of the Lord come down from heaven and cut the minister down above his feet, causing him to fall to the ground. The warning was that he had allowed pride in his heart because of his success and he must humble himself before God, or he would be "cut down" by an angel of the Lord. This was similar to the dream given to Nebuchadnezzar, twelve months before the heavenly watchers enacted the decree against him.

The minister met privately with the pastor, but the word was not well received. It was months later that he was exposed with a serious problem, which forced him to step down from the church, and for many years he was held an addictive bondage that almost cost him his life. It took many years, but over time, he received help and restoration. Later, he was able to assist a lot of young men in need, leading them on a road to deliverance.

When an Angel's Touch Becomes Deadly

After wrestling together most of the night, as the sunlight peaked across the rugged mountains, an angel touched Jacob's thigh, giving the patriarch a limp for life (Gen. 32:24–25). When an angel touched Daniel, the physically weak prophet was immediately strengthened (Dan. 10:19). When a ministering angel was released to Christ after his encounter in the wilderness with Satan and in the Garden of Gethsemane during his agony, Christ was supernaturally strengthened in both instances.

These are examples of what one touch from an angel can do. But what if the angel is sent to bring judgment instead of blessing upon a person? What can one touch from an angel do if they are assigned to bring the kiss of death to the disobedient or the wicked?

One Biblical example is found in Acts 12, when King Herod Agrippa I beheaded James and placed a death sentence upon Peter. James died a martyr. Peter, however, escaped his captors when the church prayed without ceasing and God sent a delivering angel into Peter's prison cell to remove his chains and open all the iron gates leading outside the city. God decreed that it was time to take this murderous Herod Agrippa I from the scene. An angel of God eventually enacted this death sentence.

Herod Agrippa I as a young man was sent to Rome for his formal education. He had gotten into debt but was financially bailed out by an uncle, and eventually moved to Tiberias in Israel. He was always getting into some sort of trouble. On one occasion, while he was waiting outside of a palace in chains, a strange turn of events unfolded as reported by the historian Josephus: "While waiting outside the palace in chains leaning against a tree, another prisoner, a German, saw a horned owl lighten on a tree. He then predicted to Agrippa that, in time, he would be exalted to the highest position. He also predicted the next time he would see this bird his death would follow in five days."

Six months after serving time, Agrippa was released from prison and later crowned as the king of Judea in AD 41. It was Agrippa's decree that sentenced James to execution, and when he saw it pleased many religious Jews, he arrested Peter and intended to behead him. Following Peter's supernatural release from prison, Agrippa was invited to a royal celebration on the Mediterranean coast. This is where the Biblical narrative picks up on the events that followed: "And upon a set day Herod, arrayed in royal apparel, sat upon his throne, and made an oration unto them. And the people gave a shout, saying, It is the voice of a god, and not of a man. And immediately the angel of the Lord smote him, because he gave not God the glory: and he was eaten of worms, and gave up the ghost. But the word of God grew and multiplied" (Acts 12:21–24).

According to Josephus, Agrippa came to Caesarea dressed in an outfit covered in pure shining silver. As the sun radiated off the bright metal, the people began to scream that he was a god. That is when Herod saw the same type of horned owl sitting on a rope nearby, as predicted by the German prisoner years prior. Suddenly, a pain struck him and he cried out, "I whom you call a God am now under the sentence of death." He developed severe intestinal pains and infection and died five days later at age fifty-four, after ruling for a brief seven years. Luke wrote that "the angel of the Lord smote him because he gave not God the glory and was eaten of worms and gave up the ghost" (Acts 12:22–23).

The power of one angel to strike death on a massive scale is recorded in the time of King Hezekiah, when the Assyrian army led by Sennacherib made an expedition to attack Jerusalem. The people in the city called a fast and began praying, when suddenly they received word from God through Isaiah that the Lord would defeat this army without any Israelite fighting against any Assyrian. 2 Chronicles 32:21 reads, "And the Lord sent an angel which cut off the mighty men of valor, and the leaders and captains in the camp of the Assyrians..." Isaiah gives the number of deaths in one night: "Then the angel of the LORD went out, and killed in the camp of the Assyrians one hundred and eighty-five thousand; and when people arose early in the morning, there were the corpses—all dead" (Isa. 37:36–37 NKJV).

Josephus records the details of this historic night of judgment, and identifies the cause for the numerous deaths as a "plague, for God had sent a pestilential distemper upon his army, on the very first night of the siege..." From a rabbinical perspective, this type of judgment is "death by the hand of heaven." This phrase is used when the sin against a person, or in this case against Jerusalem, is so great that God Himself becomes the judge and officiates a decree directly from His throne and commissions for a swift death to occur and assigns specific angels of judgment to enact it.

Death by the Hand of Heaven

This type of death decree can be prevented only through humility and swift repentance, as seen in the Old Testament where the offender presented a sacrifice to God to atone for the wrong. This is illustrated when David sinned by numbering the men of Israel, and did not collect the half-shekel of redemption required by Moses in the law when a census was conducted. This angered God, and He sent a plague to Israel, bringing death to 70,000 men (1 Chron. 21:14). The angel of judgment headed toward Jerusalem with his sword, and God opened David's eyes to see it. The angel instructed David to build an altar on the threshing floor on top of Mount Moriah (known today as the Temple Mount), placing an offering on the sacred altar. The fire of God fell upon the altar, and "The Lord commanded the angel, and he put up his sword again into the sheath thereof" (1 Chron. 21:26–27). The reasoning for the judgment was that when David ignored collecting the half-shekel of redemption from each man, it was as though he said that there is no price for redemption, when in reality God's son, Jesus, would one day pay the ultimate price of his life for mankind's redemption (Gal. 3:13).

Many years ago, when my dad pastored in northern Virginia, one of his members, Aaron Wright, related a fearful event he witnessed. Years prior, a church member had invited two of their neighbor's children to a local church. The mother permitted them to attend and both were touched by the Spirit of the Lord, as evidenced when they responded to the altar invitation. Suddenly, a man burst through the back doors of the church screaming, heading straight to the altar. He jerked up the two children by their arms and began cursing God and the congregation, yelling that he would not allow his children to attend this type of church, especially a "holy roller" church. When the minister told him of the verse where Jesus warned not to offend the little ones who seek him, the father reached in his pocket, held up his keys, and threatened, "The day my kids go to this church will be the day these keys will melt in hell!"

The people began weeping—the kids, too—and the father dragged them out in his pride and arrogance. A few days later, the neighbor reported back to the church that while the father was outside working, he was struck by lightning, and the most frightening part was, the lightning somehow struck the metal keys, as they were found melted in his pocket. This could never occur unless this was a direct judgment of God against a man with a reprobate mind (Romans 1).

Offending Angels

The Scripture indicates it is possible for God the Father to be grieved as He was for forty years during the Israelites' wilderness wanderings. The Holy Spirit can also be grieved as Paul wrote, "Grieve not the Holy Spirit" (Eph. 4). Even Christ felt a sense of grief, manifested when He groaned at the tomb of Lazarus, as the people did not understand His power to raise the dead (John 11:33). If the triune godhead can experience grief when men sin and disobey the Word, can angels also become grieved?

It was Solomon who wrote the following:

Keep thy foot when thou goest to the house of God, and be more ready to hear, than to give the sacrifice of fools: for they consider not that they do evil. Be not rash with thy mouth, and let not thy heart be hasty to utter anything before God: for God is in heaven, and thou upon the earth: therefore let thy words be few.... When thou vowest a vow unto God, defer not to pay it; for he has no pleasure in fools: pay which thou hast vowed. Better is it that thou shouldest not vow, than thou shouldest vow and not pay. Suffer not thy mouth to cause thy flesh to sin; neither say thou before the angel that is was an error: wherefore should God be angry at thy voice and destroy the works of thine hand. (Ecclesiastes 5:1–6)

In context, Solomon is giving instruction on preparing and following through with vows made to God, which can be conditional and unconditional oaths made in His sight. If you make a conditional oath, you bind yourself to a promise with the expectation of receiving something in return. Jacob made a vow when he promised God that if He would go with him, watch over him, and bring him back safely to the land, he would give God one-tenth of what he possessed (Gen. 22:20–22). Hannah was unable to conceive a child and vowed an oath to God that if He would give her a child, she would present him back to the Lord's service (1 Sam. 1:11).

In an unconditional oath, a person makes a promise expecting nothing in return. In apostolic times, a person who served another in a home and was given their freedom could choose to remain in the home of their master by becoming a bond servant, binding themselves to their master, expecting nothing in return. This act was done out of love for the master and his servant. Moses explained the seriousness of vows: "If a man vow a vow unto the Lord, or swear an oath to bind his soul with a bond; he shall not break his word, he shall do everything he said" (Num. 30:2).

The law of vowing emphasized that a person should always follow through with their oaths and promises. Solomon wrote that if a person speaks rashly, or in a hasty manner perhaps in anger, the angel of the Lord would become angry and destruction could follow. Judgment can be released as witnessed with Ananias and Saphirah, a couple in the Bible who pledged a specific amount to their church from a land sale. When offering time arrived, they secretly agreed to hold on to some of their earnings. They "lied to the Holy Spirit," and both were slain at the feet of the Apostle Peter (Acts 5).

Consider the promises made to God in times of crisis. A person goes to prison and promises God that if He will shorten their stay, they will "get right and stay right" with Him. A child hangs between life and death in an intensive care unit as a deadbeat dad promises God to never miss a church service as long as he lives, if He will spare his child from death. Others make outlandish "agreements" with God that if they can come into a lot of money, they will give God His well-deserved share. However, when the prisoner is released, he returns to his pigpen; when the child is cured and returns home, the absentee father is still absent. People often forget God's goodness and return to their former sinful or disobedient lives. Verbal vows are often not taken seriously.

Solomon wrote that if we make a rash vow, the "angel will destroy the works of our hands." The word "destroy" used in Ecclesiastes means "to wind tight like a rope or to bind." This implies that the angel of God can make success difficult, or restrain the blessing of the works of a person's hands. For example, after Israel returned from Babylon, the former captives ignored the needs to restore and rebuild the Temple, and concentrated only on their personal monetary status. This resulted in economic distress for the people. Haggai described the situation as putting money in a bag with holes in it. God also reminded the people that He controlled the rain and could open or close the heavens, causing either drought or prosperity (Hag. 1:6; Mal. 3:8–11).

When Israel departed from Egypt and traveled en masse to the Promised Land, a powerful angel was continually with them. God warned Israel not to provoke this heavenly messenger:

> Behold, I send an Angel before thee, to keep thee in the way, and to bring thee into the place which I have prepared. Beware of him, and obey his voice, provoke him not; for he will not pardon your transgressions: for my name is in him. But if thou shalt indeed obey his voice, and do all that I speak; then I will be an enemy unto thine enemies, and an adversary unto thine adversaries. For mine angel shall go before thee... (Exodus 23:20–23)

This angel, called the "Angel of His presence" (Exod. 33:14), was concealed in the cloud during the day and in the fire by night to observe the people continually (Num. 20:16). The sacred name of God was attached to this angel, to the point that if the people provoked him, he would hold their disobedience against them. For this reason, when the ten spies corrupted the entire Israelite camp with unbelief, God sent the entire nation back into the wilderness for forty years, and they were not given a second chance to repent and enter the land. God had warned them the angel of His presence would not forgive them if they offended him. The numerous complaints of the multitude mixed with their unbelief toward God's promises caused a delay in God's purpose for forty years.

For a believer, one of our greatest sins is unbelief; it limits or refuses to believe in the supernatural power and manifestations of God. It is sad to hear individuals who read the same Bible take verses out of context to say that God no longer performs miracles; there are sixty-six books filled with miracles. Do not expect any type of angelic manifestation when a person is filled with unbelief and doubt. The angel of God's presence saw and heard the unbelief of the people, and sent them in circles for forty years.

21 UNUSUAL AND CONTROVERSIAL QUESTIONS ABOUT ANGELS ANSWERED

1. Should we ever pray directly to an angel?

The Bible instructs all believers how to pray, and in no Biblical instance did a person pray directly to an angel unless the "angel of the Lord" was the Lord Himself. For example, when Abraham stood in the gap of intercession for Lot, who was living in the doomed city of Sodom, the Bible says, "The Lord and two angels" were involved in the decision. Abraham began negotiating with the Lord for the numbers of souls required to spare the city from its complete destruction (Gen. 18).

Under the New Covenant, we are to petition the Heavenly Father using the authority of the name of Jesus Christ (John 16:23). Christ said to ask in His name and we would receive, that our joy may be full (John 16:24). Nowhere, and at no time from Adam to John the Apostle, did a godly person pray in the name of some angel. From the time of Moses on, it was common for men to pray in the name of the God of "Abraham, Isaac, and Jacob" (Exod. 32:13; Lev. 26:42; Deut. 9:27; 1 Kings 18:36). In the New Testament, prayers are said in the name of Christ, including prayers for salvation (Acts 2:38) and healing (Acts 3:6; James 5:14), and all prayers were to be spoken in the name of Jesus Christ, as this was required to approach the throne of God.

This is perhaps the reason that only two angels are mentioned in Scripture: Gabriel and Michael (Luke 1:19; Rev. 12: Jude 9). There are older mainline churches that at times tend to bring attention to both of these angels. If the Lord mentioned all of the unnamed angels in Scripture, it is quite possible, knowing the nature of men, that some form of angelic worship would have emerged in the church. The name of Christ is the only name under heaven whereby man can be saved (Acts 4:12).

2. Should an angel ever receive worship?

One of the most interesting aspects of angels appearing in human form is the manner in which people responded to them. They often "fell on the ground" out of fear or awe (Josh. 5:14; Judg. 13:20; Ezek. 1:25–28; Dan. 10:5–9). When the guards at Christ's tomb saw the angels appear, they "became as dead men" (Matt. 28:4). When the Lord appeared to the patriarchs, they would often fall prostrate and worship the Lord. When John saw Christ in a vision, he fell to the ground, and throughout

Revelation, the twenty-four elders fall on their faces to worship the lamb (Rev. 5:8, 14; 7:11; 11:16; 19:4).

There are instances in which individuals saw an "angel of the Lord" and, after realizing it was an angel, were afraid they would die. When Gideon understood he had encountered an angel "face to face," the angel comforted him by telling him he would not die (Judg. 6:22–23). In Judges 13, the mother of Samson saw an angel who refused to tell her his name, which was a "secret" (Judg. 13:18). When the angel ascended in a flame from the altar, Manoah said to his wife, "We will surely die because we have seen God" (Judg. 13:22). She reminded him that the angel said they would have a son that would be delivered in Israel, and if the angel wanted to kill them, he already would have! When the "angel" was perceived as the "Lord," then it received worship, as when the Lord and two angels appeared at Abraham's tent (Gen. 18). However, when clearly an angel of the Lord, it refused worship.

The best example is found when an angel of the Lord showed John the entire vision penned in the book of Revelation. John wrote: "The Lord God of the holy prophets sent His angel to show His servants the things that must shortly be done" (Rev. 22:6). At the conclusion of the vision, John went to worship the angel and was forbidden: "Now I, John, saw and heard these things. And when I heard and saw, I fell down to worship before the feet of the angel who showed me these things. Then he said to me, 'See that you do not do that. For I am your fellow servant, and of your brethren the prophets, and of those who keep the words of this book. Worship God'" (Rev. 22:8–9 NKJV).

This angel who unlocked the apocalypse to John rejected his

worship and told him to "worship God." Any true angel of the Lord would never allow himself to be worshipped, as they know that God alone is to be praised and worshipped.

Based on Ezekiel 28:13–15, Satan was a cherub whose brightness and beauty lifted his heart in pride. He desired to sit in the mountain of the congregation (where God is worshipped) and "be like the Most High" (Isa. 14:13–14). One of the three temptations of Christ was Satan's offering for Jesus to "bow and worship him" (Matt. 4:9), in return for world power. This statement reveals the true intent of Satan, which is to receive worship and adoration as God does. There is a difference between worshipping God, who is "worthy," and Satan, who has never accomplished one noteworthy event since his expulsion from heaven.

3. Do we have authority to command angels to do assignments for us?

In Scripture, the decrees and the instructions for angels are given by God Himself, as psalm 91:11 indicates, "He [God] will give His angels charge over you." Some people teach that we as believers should pray to angels and ask them to do all sorts of helpful activities for us. First of all, God will never *do for us* what we can *do for ourselves*. He does not plant money trees on earth that we can pluck cash from like apples, but blesses the works of our hands (Deut. 15:10). God gave Moses the plan for the tabernacle, but Moses and the people constructed the entire tent with offerings of various metals and animal skins that people provided (Exod. 25–39). Notice, however, when there was a need, such as the wine shortage at the wedding and lack of food to feed 5,000 men and their families, God intervened supernaturally. Jesus provided the water, and God provided the wine. Jesus provided the five loaves and two fish, and God provided a mass feeding with twelve baskets left over (John 3:2–10; Matt. 14:17–20).

Angels are assigned by God and, at times, are under the authority of higher-ranking angels, such as Michael (Rev. 12:7–10). If we sense there is a need for a divine intervention, or are in a dangerous or life-threatening situation, or have an extreme need, we can ask God to bring angelic assistance on our behalf.

I recall when our ministry was building the OCI gathering place to reach youth. We knew we were in the will of God, but we also knew we were short millions of dollars required to pay for the facility. I knew that there were finances out there that could be applied to this project, and I remember requesting the prayer team to ask the Lord to send an angel to awaken the spirit of a millionaire and give him either a dream or a revelation to assist us. I had no one in mind, but we prayed earnestly that God would assist us supernaturally. Within a few months, we were receiving million-dollar checks from an unknown source (a charitable trust) that helped us pay off the facility.

Sometimes, a person who may not be in covenant with God will have an encounter with an angel of the Lord in a dream, or be given an impression to do something. Remember, the dream given to Pharaoh that warned of the coming seven-year famine, and Nebuchadnezzar's dream of a man made of metal, which revealed the empires, were two of the greatest prophetic dreams in the Bible. At the time of these dreams, neither king was a convert of the true God and it required two men filled with the Holy Spirit—Joseph and Daniel—to interpret them (Gen. 41; Dan. 2). Angels' food came from heaven to earth for forty years to feed Israel, and angels can also assist in our provisional needs.

Years ago, we were preparing a satellite feed around the world for our home television studio. One hour before, there was a serious problem that seemed impossible to fix. My father went into the prayer room and fervently began interceding that the angels of the Lord would restrain every hindering spirit in the atmosphere who was assigned to our program. Just prior to the starting time, the bad weather ceased, our equipment suddenly began working, and we began on time. We all knew it would take divine intervention to move our plans forward, and we indeed received special help from above! There are times in extreme emergencies, dangerous situations, and hindrances when it is possible to ask the Father in heaven for angelic assistance.

4. Are angels with us continually, or only during difficult seasons?

I believe angels have *access* to us continually, but are not necessarily constantly with us, as the Holy Spirit is the other comforter who will "abide with you forever" (John 14:16) and "dwell with you and shall be in you" (John 14:17). The Holy Spirit has provided prayer language for every Spirit-filled believer, enabling them to pray for the perfect will of God (Rom. 8:26–28), and for Him to intercede when they're burdened or in need. The Holy Spirit assists us in worship, prayer, and understanding the Word of God and life in general. Paul wrote that it is possible to pray in the "tongues of men and of angels" (1 Cor. 13:1), implying that there is a language that angels communicate in that may not be the same as what we use on earth.

The prayer language of the Holy Spirit is our spirit praying to God (1 Cor. 14:4); however, it is possible that the Holy Spirit can and does call on angelic assistance at times. Here's why: God works *in* us and the angels work on the *outside* realm. The Holy Spirit moves upon the heart and the *inner* spirit of a person, whereas angels can work through *outward* circumstances, as they exercise more contact within the natural world, and can be sent from one situation to another. To put it another way, the Holy Spirit's ministry is *inward* and the angelic ministry is *outward*. Angels are not needed every day, but the Holy Spirit is with us every day. When Peter's chains needed to be broken and the prison door opened, an angel was sent (Acts 12:7). An angel was required to appear to Cornelius, as he was not yet filled with the Holy Spirit to direct him inwardly. Thus, the angel placed him with Peter and the Holy Spirit did the rest of the work as Peter preached the Word. Notice in Acts 10:44–47, the phrase "Holy Ghost" (KJV) is mentioned three times (vv. 44, 45, and 47). The angel is the key messenger in the beginning of chapter 10 (vv. 3 and 7), and the Holy Spirit is the main messenger at the conclusion of the narrative.

In the temptation of Christ, the Holy Spirit led Him into the wilderness to be tested by the devil for forty days (Luke 4:1). The Holy Spirit came upon Christ at His Baptism and was with Him from that moment onward, never leaving Him and anointing His ministry (Acts 10:38). However, when Christ was at His weakest moments (during the temptation and also in Gethsemane), angels were commissioned to give Him strength (Matt. 4:11; Luke 22:43). There is no record that the angels were with Him throughout the temptation, or during His three hours in the garden. They appeared at a specific moment of need, briefly ministered strength and encouragement, and then departed. The Holy Spirit is with us always, but angels minister in specific seasons of need.

5. If we sin, are angels watching us, and what happens if they are?

When Israel departed from Egypt, there was an angel of God's presence who dwelt in the cloud that followed the people for forty years. God told them that it was "His angel" and warned that if the people sinned and the angel saw it, He would not forgive them: "Behold, I send an Angel before you to keep you in the way and to bring you into the place which I have prepared. Beware of Him and obey His voice; do not provoke Him, for He will not pardon your transgressions; for My name is in Him" (Exod. 23:20–22 NKJV).

Israel's sin was unbelief. Ten spies convinced the multitude they could not take the Promised Land, and the people wandered in the wilderness for forty years—one year for each day the spies were in the land (Num. 14:34). Israel also worshipped the golden calf (Exod. 32:4–20), seen by both God and the angel. Who was this special angel who possessed the name of the Lord?

When the forty years expired, the cloud ceased and Joshua saw this angel near Jericho. The angel told Joshua he was "Captain of the Lord of hosts" (Josh. 5:14). Some suggest this was actually Michael the archangel. The word "captain" in Hebrew here is *sar,* meaning a chief, ruler, or prince. Michael is called the prince that stands for Israel using the same language in Daniel 12:1. The word for "hosts" in Joshua 5:14 is the Hebrew *tsaba',* meaning a mass of persons or things organized for war, and can allude to soldiers or an army. In this case the army would be the angels who battle on behalf of the people of God! It is possible this angel was a manifestation of Michael, visible in human form, who was assisting Israel in the upcoming supernatural victory in Jericho.

God said His name was in the name of the angel. The Hebrew version of Michael is *Miyka'el,* which means, "who is like God." The term *el* at the end is an early Hebrew name for God, and comes from a root word meaning "might strength and power." Both Michael and Gabriel have "el" in their names, which possibly indicates that the name of God is concealed within the name of His chief angels. God told Moses that His angel would go before them into battle against the seven tribes that were controlling the land: "For My Angel will go before you and bring you in to the Amorites and the Hittites and the Perizzites and the Canaanites and the Hivites and the Jebusites; and I will cut them off" (Exod. 23:23–24).

God the Father, Christ, the Holy Spirit, and—yes—any angel connected to a person is aware of sin. This is why it is important to repent and keep a humble spirit before the Lord always, and never harden your heart as the Israelites did in the wilderness.

The generation that was liberated from bondage ended up dying in a dry desert instead of enjoying their inheritance.

6. How could a demon prince spirit stop Gabriel for twenty-one days (Daniel 10)? Aren't angels more powerful than that?

The answer to this lies in realm of authority. God delegates authority to specific individuals. Adam, for example, was given "dominion" over the entire animal kingdom, and to this day, man rules over all the animals on earth (Gen. 1:26–28). During the temptation of Christ, Satan offered Him the "kingdoms of the world" if He would worship him, but Christ refused. Satan bragged that the world's kingdoms had been delivered unto him and he would give them to "whomever he desired" (Luke 4:5–6). The authority to dominate world governments was a part of what Satan received after the fall of Adam, as Satan is presently the illegitimate "god of this world" (2 Cor. 4:4). He is not the god of the earth itself, which is the Lord's (1 Cor. 10:26), but he reigns over the world's system of thinking, false religions, and evil and corruption that dominate ungodly governments.

Angels are given specific assignments and varied levels of authority. It is believed the angel carrying the prophetic revelation to Daniel was Gabriel, who is not a warring angel but one whose main messages directly concern prophetic movements on earth. When Gabriel was entering the atmosphere over Babylon, the leading spirit over Persia intercepted and restrained him in a sort of cosmic wrestling match for three weeks. To break this hindrance, God commissioned Michael, heaven's warring angel and the chief guardian over Israel (Dan. 12:1) to hold back the demonic prince of Persia. He wrestled Satan to prevent him from seizing the corpse of Moses (Jude 9), and will in the future battle Satan and his angels, expelling them from the second heaven to earth in the middle of the tribulation (Rev. 12:7–10).

When Michael rebuked Satan in the valley of Pisgah during the battle for Moses' body, he rebuked Satan by saying, "the Lord rebuke you" (Jude 9). The same words are used in Zechariah 3, where an "angel of the Lord" stands beside the high priest, with Satan on the right side of the altar to resist the priest (Zech. 3:1–2). These angels understand that they are representing the authority of God Himself, and when they rebuke Satan in the Lord's name, Satan has no authority to resist them.

Gabriel's need for assistance may be due to the fact that he is not a warrior, but a messenger. When the last cosmic war convenes in Revelation 12, it is with "Michael and his angels" (v. 7). Michael's angels are obviously warring spirits that do battle against the forces of darkness. Gabriel's authority rests in his revelations given to people on earth on numerous occasions, whereas Michael's authority is to directly deal with Satan and his kingdom. For example, I am a minister and not in authority in any military realm. If I went to Israel and attempted to cross the border as a "minister," they would stop me. However, if I cross with the authority of a high-ranking military escort, I pass easily because the men with me have the authority to cross borders. Michael has a high level of warring power, and

Gabriel, a high level of revelatory authority. When a demonic prince given authority over an entire nation stopped Gabriel from entering its domain, Michael, who is of superior authority as he dominates the guardianship of Israel, intervened. Since Daniel's vision concerned the future of Israel, Michael had the "legal authority" to enter the realm of Babylon, allowing Gabriel to bring the answer Daniel was seeking.

7. Can angels at times appear to look like our family members?

This may be one of the biggest scriptural mysteries for several reasons. Spirits can actually take on different forms in their realm. We know that angels are spirits, and to the human eye, they are invisible; yet in their own realm, they can be seen by all other spirits on the same level. Satan is not invisible to God, the Holy Spirit, Christ, or other angelic beings, just as God is not invisible to all forms of demonic agents.

Angels have taken on forms of men, to the point that humans were unable to distinguish that they were actually angels, as was the case when the angels entered Lot's house (Gen. 19). When the Holy Spirit descended upon Christ, the Bible says He came "like a dove" (Matt. 3:16). Luke added more detail when he wrote, "And the Holy Spirit descended in the bodily shape like a dove" (Luke 3:22). All four gospel writers indicate this was the Holy Spirit and not just a manifestation (Matt. 3:16; Mark 1:10; Luke 3:22; John 1:32). We assume the Holy Spirit has some type of bodily form, such as a head, hands, feet, and so forth, as God, who is a spirit

(John 4:24), is noted to have hands, feet, eyes, ears, and other features, like man, who was created in His image (Gen. 1:26–27).

Spirits are in a completely different dimension than humans, and with their ability to travel at the speed of thought, they can create the appearance of light, brightness, and fire. One logical reason for invisibility is that the speed at which they travel is too fast for human eyes. We would have to have a veil lifted to be able to see the upper realms.

There have been numerous accounts from people who believed they encountered an angel who had a very similar appearance to a person they were close to in this life. In some instances, the images were part of a vision a believer experienced. It is unclear from Scripture how or why an angel would take on a certain physical likeness, but we do know that nothing is impossible with God. Angels can appear and be fearful to look upon to some. Samson's mother saw an angel and described it as "very terrible" (Judg. 13:6) or, as some translate, "very awesome" to look upon (Judg. 13:6). The actual Hebrew word here translated as "terrible" is *yare'* and can mean "to frighten" or "frightening." Perhaps the Lord sends angels, whether in dreams or visions, to a person in a similar appearance to a loved one in order to bring peace and comfort.

8. Are some UFO sightings possibly linked with angelic activity, such as Ezekiel's "wheel"?

There has been a fascination with UFOs (unidentified flying objects) since their first alleged appearance in the 1940s.

The majority of those in the West see these objects as nothing more than secret U.S. military projects to spy on other nations. Others suspect some form of alien life is visiting our planet in spaceships, using advanced technology unknown to our scientists. Others believe these images and round disks called flying saucers are visible manifestations of something from the spirit world, similar to what the prophet Ezekiel attempted to describe in a vision.

The Biblical book of Ezekiel opens with the prophet explaining a vision of God, where a fiery whirlwind that contained four living creatures approached him from the north. The creatures, who traveled at the speed of lightning (Ezek. 1:1–14), were actually angels called cherubim, each with four wings on their sides and four faces: a man, an ox, a lion, and an eagle. One section of Ezekiel's vision alludes to "wheels": "Now as I looked at the living creatures, behold, a wheel was on the earth beside each living creature with its four faces. The appearance of the wheels and their workings was like the color of beryl, and all four had the same likeness. The appearance of their workings was, as it were, a wheel in the middle of a wheel" (Ezek. 1:15–17 NKJV).

Also note Ezekiel 1:18–21:

As for their rims, they were so high they were awesome; and their rims were full of eyes, all around the four of them. When the living creatures went, the wheels went beside them; and when the living creatures were lifted up from the earth, the wheels were lifted up. Wherever the spirit wanted to go, they went, because there the spirit went; and the wheels were lifted together with them, for the spirit of the living creatures was in the wheels. When those went, these went; when those stood, these stood; and when those were lifted up from the earth, the wheels were lifted up together with them, for the spirit of the living creatures was in the wheels. (NKJV)

Much can be said about the details of these angelic beings. However, the central subject matter is the "wheels within the wheels." Let's assume that a man from 2,800 years ago is describing a flying craft, similar to the circular UFOs that have been photographed. How would he describe the lights around the edges of the vehicle? Would he see them as "eyes" instead of lights, since lights did not exist 2,800 years ago? What is the "wheel within the wheel"? Would this be the circular dome that is in the center of a flying craft? Since a craft moves up, down, forward, and sideways very quickly, would the prophet assume that the life force of the object is in its center?

What I have described to you is the theory of some Christian UFO enthusiasts to explain the vision of Ezekiel: The prophet was seeing an alien spacecraft or a UFO, and was attempting to give a description to the people. It is easy to read Ezekiel once and, using one's imagination, create a scenario in which the prophet is seeing an object from outer space manifest on the earth, then fly with lightning speed back into the upper atmosphere.

However, when we compare all the verses in Ezekiel 1–10, the prophet is clearly describing cherubim, a particular type of angel who, in his vision, is transporting the throne of God through the heavens toward the Jews in captivity in Babylon. God sits on the throne and appears as fire (Ezek. 1:26–27). According to rabbinical sources, the "wheels" are the movement of the four living creatures carrying God's throne. This is called the Merkabah, or when the throne of God becomes His chariot. This may be what David alluded to when he wrote, "God rode upon a Cherub and did fly and was seen upon the wings of the wing" (2 Sam. 22:11).

It is a far stretch of the imagination for someone to interpret these passages as unidentified flying objects. However, to say they are "from another world" is correct, but the world is not a realm of space aliens—it is the amazing realm of angels.

9. Why do some angels appear at times as children?

While there is not any Scripture where angels appear as children, there are countless stories of children appearing to believers who were, in reality, angelic visitors. The concept of children as angels is often connected with the Scriptures that Christ spoke of, where the angels of children behold the face of the Father in heaven (Matt. 18:10). In medieval times, it was common for artists to paint infants with wings, or "baby cherubim," as some believed that when an infant died, their spirit was transformed into a baby angel. When David's infant son (the child of Bathsheba) died seven days after his birth, David said he could not bring him back, but would instead go where the child was. He was not speaking of going to the grave, but was alluding to paradise, where the righteous souls go after death (2 Sam. 12:23). The spirit of the child had departed from his body and was with other righteous souls in paradise. He was not transformed into an angelic being, but will be raised at the resurrection of the dead and given an immortal body in the future, as will David and all righteous souls who died in covenant with God and Christ.

It is a bit difficult to explain angels who appear as children, as Scripture is silent on this subject. In all angelic appearances to people and in dreams and visions, the angel always appeared as a man. The only example of an angel looking like a woman is when Zechariah describes angels carrying a woman in a basket to the land of Shinar: "Then I raised my eyes and looked, and there were two women, coming with the wind in their wings; for they had wings like the wings of a stork, and they lifted up the basket between earth and heaven" (Zech. 5:9).

There are numerous mysteries connected to the realm of spirits, both evil and angelic. One moment, they can appear in spirit form, and other times as a "man." Other times, they manifest in a dream or a vision, with bright white remnants or in a flaming fire. These various forms give us a clue that angels can change their appearance. Because of this unique ability, there is the possibility they can appear in younger forms, such as a child, but only if there is a specific purpose for this kind of manifestation.

10. Paul said we would judge the angels: "Do you not know that we shall judge angels?" (1 Corinthians 6:3). How is that possible, and what will they be judged for?

In this verse, Paul is reprimanding believers for taking other believers to court before ungodly judges. He reminds the church at Corinth that we will one day judge the world (1 Cor. 6:2), and tells them to find wise men in the church to handle their legal matters (1 Cor. 6:5).

There are two major judgments in heaven. The first is found in Revelation 11:18, identified as the "Bema," or the judgment seat of Christ, where all believers will stand before Him and be judged for their words, actions, and works. Either they will receive rewards or they won't, based upon the outcome of the judgment. The second instance is the "great white throne judgment" at the end of the thousand-year reign of Christ, when all people from the beginning of time, including spirits assigned to hell, the fallen angels, and Satan and his demonic hosts will be judged (Rev. 20:11–15). The fallen angels are those who followed Satan in the great cosmic rebellion prior to the creation of Adam (Luke 10:18). Peter wrote that these angels sinned and were "cast down into hell, and delivered into chains of darkness, to be reserved unto judgment" (2 Pet. 2:4).

Thus, there are two groups of angels: one-third, who reside in hell with Satan (Rev. 12:4), and the other two-thirds, who remain loyal to God. It is likely that the angels referred to here are the fallen ones who sinned and are chained in the lowest hell (called Tartarus in Greek in 2 Peter 2:4) and are being reserved for the day of the final judgment. Jude also wrote about these fallen angels and said: "And the angels who did not keep their proper domain, but left their own abode, He has reserved in everlasting chains under darkness for the judgment of the great day" (Jude 6).

These are the angels the saint will judge at the great white throne. After, "death and hell were cast into the lake of fire" (Rev. 20:14). The Bible tells us that the "books will be opened" and the "dead were judged out of those things written in the books" (Rev. 20:12). God certainly has heavenly records of the actions or deeds of these angels, and before being cast into the eternal lake of fire, along with Satan, they will be judged by the records and condemned for their actions. God, being a righteous judge, will never confine anyone into an eternal prison unless they see the evidence that is against them in a heavenly court.

11. Can certain animals sense or see angels if they are in a room?

This is an interesting question. We know from Scripture that humans have some type of a veil or covering over their eyes that prevents them from seeing all types of spirits, including angels. Only when this covering is lifted can a person see the invisible. When Elisha prayed, the eyes of his servant opened to see the chariots and horses of fire (2 Kings 6:15–17). Elisha himself was supernaturally able to see Elijah's angelic transportation to heaven, when the other fifty sons of the prophets standing at a distance saw nothing but a whirlwind (2 Kings 2). When Christ was raised from the grave, He appeared to two men with veiled eyes who did not recognize Him. Only when the veil was removed did they realize they were speaking to Christ (Luke 24:13–31).

It may be that this veil hiding the spirit world from human eyes is a part of our sin nature that was initiated at the fall. When Adam sinned, he could still hear the voice of God in the garden, but people would no longer see God face-to-face in fellowship (Gen. 3). When Adam and Eve sinned, a series of curses was initiated, but the only curse placed on the animal kingdom was upon the serpent, who was doomed "above all cattle and above every beast of the field" (Gen. 3:14). The animals, cattle, and other "beasts" had no sin nature and were therefore incapable of sinning.

This is important to note when Balaam rode his donkey to the top of a mountain in Moab to place a curse on Israel. The Lord instructed him not to go, but the seer rebelled and continued on his way. Moses wrote that God sent an angel to block Balaam's path. The oddity is that the donkey clearly saw the angel and Balaam saw nothing. The donkey refused to move forward, and actually crushed Balaam's foot against a rock at one point:

> And the ass saw the angel of the LORD standing in the way, and his sword drawn in his hand: and the ass turned aside out of the way, and went into the field: and Balaam smote

the ass, to turn her into the way. But the angel of the LORD stood in a path of the vineyards, a wall being on this side, and a wall on that side. And when the ass saw the angel of the LORD, she thrust herself unto the wall, and crushed Balaam's foot against the wall: and he smote her again. And the angel of the LORD went further, and stood in a narrow place, where was no way to turn either to the right hand or to the left. And when the ass saw the angel of the LORD, she fell down under Balaam: and Balaam's anger was kindled, and he smote the ass with a staff. (Numbers 22:23–27)

Three separate times the donkey saw the angel and not once did Balaam. Nowhere does the passage say that the Lord opened the eyes of the donkey to see the angel. This is the only place in Scripture where an animal visibly sees an angel, and apparently thinks a man is standing in his path.

This one verse in no way proves that when an angel is present, animals can sense it. However, there are too many stories to tell where certain animals inside a home can at times sense both a good and an evil presence within the home. Dogs have a keen sense of smell and also are able to sense fear, anger, and grief in their owners. There have been times when animals have acted in a peculiar manner, as though something is troubling them or they are sensing someone in the room. It is possible that, at times, some animals can sense the presence of angelic and even demonic spirits.

12. Can I ask angels to protect my children when they travel?

I began traveling as a full-time evangelist at age eighteen, and sometimes drove as far as Long Island, New York, to minister. This was before GPS, cell phones, or electronic emergency devices in cars. When I was traveling, all I had was a letter from the pastor of the church where I was headed, a map, and quarters to use at a phone booth if I needed to call for more directions or in an emergency.

Each time I packed my car, my father continually prayed for my protection until he passed away. I often heard him ask God to "let an angel accompany Perry wherever he goes." Many times I would close out a revival on Saturday night, drive all night after service, and arrive at the next speaking location in another state early the next morning. This was unwise, but I was in high demand and was used to staying up late at night. Of course, this was of no comfort to Dad, who would sit in a chair or kneel in the early hours of the morning asking God to keep me awake and watch over me.

Early one Sunday morning in 1980, I left Tuscaloosa, Alabama, to head to Jackson, Mississippi, about a two-and-a-half-hour drive. I remember being so sleepy as I set my cruise control at 65 mph headed down I-20. I was to minister that Sunday morning and had no choice but to drive without a "rest stop." About thirty minutes into the drive, I literally nodded off to sleep. I don't know how many seconds passed, but suddenly a hand from "someone" in the backseat struck me on the right shoulder, jarring me awake. I had already drifted left off the road and in front of me was the corner of a bridge, which I swerved to miss. If another second had passed, I would have crashed into the concrete and no doubt been killed.

I began to tremble and cry because I knew an angel of the Lord had struck me to wake me up. The circumstances were different, but I was reminded of the time Peter was in prison and was sound asleep, and the angel of the Lord "smote Peter on the side and raised him up" (Acts 12:7). In many instances throughout my life when a dangerous or life-threatening situation occurred, there was always someone who had been burdened to pray for me at the very moment when the danger manifested.

Losing an Engine on the Plane

Several years ago, my pilot, Kevin Wright, flew on a clear Sunday night to Madisonville, Kentucky, to pick me up and head back to Chattanooga. At 13,000 feet in the air, and about twenty minutes from the Chattanooga airport, I suddenly heard a strange sound and felt the plane pull to the left. Through the headset Kevin said, "What was that?" Our 421 airplane had twin piston engines and the monitor on the dash indicated the left engine had gone out. We were suddenly flying on one engine, not knowing why the left one had died. Great fear overcame me and I began to wonder if the right engine would soon go, too. In the dark and surrounded by mountains, the likelihood of a safe landing with a double engine loss was virtually nil. It would mean death to both Kevin and me.

I knew I had to fight fear, and began to pray and ask God for help. While Kevin called in an emergency, I asked the Lord in fear and trembling to send his protective angels, one at the nose of the plane and one at the tail section, to guide us safely to the airport. Kevin made all the correct emergency decisions, and after a rather hard landing, the crippled plane slowly made its way to the hangar.

Later I discovered that three people were praying at the same time—two of whom knew nothing about the engine loss, but felt a strong sense that we were in danger and they should intercede. Kevin's wife asked him when he got home, "What happened tonight? When you left to pick up Perry, I was so burdened I haven't stopped praying and knew something was going to happen!" The next morning, my head prayer intercessor, Bea Ogle, asked, knowing nothing, what happened at about 11:15 last night. I told her about the plane and she said, "The Lord told me you were in danger, and I prayed for about an hour for protection before I felt relief."

In this situation, several people at one time were praying for angelic protection. Although no one saw an angel, a safe landing that could have been harmed by one wrong move leads me to believe God sent His heavenly agents of protection to assist us to safety.

Why Do Some Live and Others Do Not?

After any tragedy or death by natural disaster, people ask, "Why did some good people survive and others did not?" This is a very challenging question to answer, but I have two examples that may shed some light. In Acts 12, Herod arrested two apostles, James and Peter. Herod was intent on killing both, and succeeded in beheading James, putting Peter on the death list. When Peter was chained up in the prison, the church prayed ceaselessly for him to be spared. It may be that James's arrest and beheading was so swift that the church had no time for deep intercession, and upon hearing of Peter's death sentence, they united in unwavering prayer, and an angel rescued Peter from being slain.

A second reason for Peter's life extension may be the fact that Christ predicted that Peter would be led to his death at an old age (John 21:18). When Herod arrested Peter, the rugged fisherman was still young, but many years later, Peter was arrested and crucified. Thus, God's plan for Peter was not completed and prayer released the angel to deliver him so he could continue his apostolic ministry.

The second example involves John the Baptist. His assignment was to be the forerunner to Christ and herald the announcement that the Messiah had come. However, John was arrested and violently beheaded by Herod near the beginning of Christ's ministry. He did, however, say that he must decrease and Christ must increase (John 3:30). When Christ heard that John was arrested, He could have helped secure John's freedom or perform a miracle for him, implied in Matthew 11:2–6. It was time for John's ministry to cease and Christ's to begin. Many of John's followers became Christ's followers.

There will be occasions in life in which there is not an answer for what happened. When Oral Roberts began teaching on how to pray a hedge around your family, his own daughter and son-in-law were killed in a small plane accident. When he cried out to God for an answer, the Lord spoke to him that there were things about their deaths that he would never understand in this life, but would be made clear to him when he went home to be with the Lord.

As for protective angels, there are two ways they are released into a situation. One is by the sovereign will of God, in which He directs the assignment to fulfill His perfect will. The other is when prayer intercedes as believers ask God for that assistance. Why does it require us asking or praying, and why doesn't God just send angels without our asking? This would be like asking: Why doesn't God just save people from sin without asking, or heal the sick without them believing God is able, or fill people with the Spirit automatically without asking for it? The simple answer is there is a law of the Spirit and the Word that says God at times will do nothing until He is asked, as asking requires faith. The law of answered prayer works on the law of faith: asking and believing before receiving. Asking also demonstrates our dependency on God instead of our own ability.

We do what we can and God does what we cannot. My pilot was trained for an engine loss, but because of the type of plane we were flying in, we know God intervened in our safety as prayer was offered for "protection." Remember, when the enemy has a plan, prayer is what can restrain it from being initiated. Jesus warned Peter that Satan desired to "sift him as wheat." Then Jesus said, "But I have prayed for you that your faith will not fail" (Luke 22:31–32). Never minimize the effective prayers of a righteous person to prevent the strategy of Satan from coming to pass, and never underestimate the ability of the angels of God to protect you from danger, "for the angel of the Lord encamps around all those that fear Him and delivers them" (Ps. 34:7).

13. How can we discern when an angel is in a room, or when we are in the presence of an angel?

In 1 Corinthians 12:7–10, there is a list of nine spiritual gifts given to the Body of Christ. One such gift is "discerning of spirits." Often in charismatic circles, believers assume this gift is only to detect the evil or unclean spirits possessing people before expelling them through prayer. Notice "spirits" is plural. This gift assists in detecting the unseen motives and intents of a person (what is in their spirit), as well as the presence of evil spirits as Christ did (Luke 13:11–16) and the presence of angels.

In the Bible, when angels were seen, there was an overpowering presence of God and a holy reverence that often overwhelmed people, causing them to fall prostrate. During my lifetime I have experienced the presence of angels. Many people have asked what it was like and how I knew it was an angel.

First of all, the location in which the Divine Presence is sensed is important. The Holy Spirit lives within us and His activity moves inward to outward. When we pray in the Spirit, our (inward) spirit is praying (1 Cor. 14:14). As Christ taught, the river of life flows out of our "belly" or inward man (John 7:38). When an angel enters a room, the presence is around you and not just in you. The entire atmosphere shifts, and there is always a strong sense of the holiness of God. In nearly every angelic visitation I've experienced, I began to cry and felt as though I should not move. Those who have known our ministry for years have on occasions been in a service where we know God had sent an angel into our presence. It is so evident that even those who are a bit more skeptical are seen trembling, weeping, or in awe. Some (such as my father) would describe it like invisible electricity in the air. I am sure this is because these spiritual agents have been in God's presence and they carry it with them.

The second "change" I have always sensed is a peace that settles over the room and myself. If your spirit is troubled, there will be the most marvelous sense of peace that will "charge" the room. When this peace manifests, there is not a care in life that is stronger than what you feel. It is as though everything melts away.

The third point would be there is also a unique strength that replaces any fatigue or weakness of the mind, spirit, or flesh when the angelic presence departs. On several occasions I was so physically exhausted from ministering that I was uncertain if I could carry on. Suddenly I felt that outward presence and knew an angel of God was visiting. Once the presence lifted, a new strength settled over me. There was mental clarity, spiritual renewal, and physical strength. I can assure you that when you are in the presence of the Divine, you will know, as it will be pleasantly different from anything you have experienced before.

14. When an angel is present, can we, at times, smell a special fragrance?

The Scripture makes reference to a "sweet smelling savor" (Exod. 29:41) when sacrifices were offered on the brass altar. Paul also marked the financial offerings of the church as "an odor of a sweet smell, a sacrifice acceptable" (Phil. 4:18). There are numerous Jewish traditions that indicate that the incense burnt on the golden altar inside the holy place filled the sacred house with a beautiful fragrance.

There have been many individuals who have experienced moments when a very strange yet sweet, pleasant odor filled a room where someone was about to pass away, or when the presence of God was strong through prayer.

Some time ago, I experienced the oddest manifestation in my ministry. I was preaching four services in two days in a high school auditorium in Logan, West Virginia. Each time I entered the building through the hallway, I smelled roses. No one else could detect the scent, except on one occasion when it was very strong. We suspected someone was spraying a fragrance, but nothing was ever found. Then I smelled the exact same odor in my hotel room—like flowers in a funeral home. Only I could sense it, which to me was some type of "sign" I needed to discern. I began to feel this was a warning of a premature death that I needed to pray against, and because only I could smell the roses, it was someone connected to my family.

I prayed against the spirit of death and asked God to send His angel to protect whoever was in danger. A few days later,

I received a call that my mother had gone home from work for lunch and fallen in the house, breaking her ankle and left wrist. When I got to the hospital, Mom explained she'd slipped in the kitchen, and was bleeding and could not get up off the floor. The pain was unbearable, but she managed to reach her new cell phone, which she had in her pocket, to call 911. The paramedics broke through the back door, stopped the bleeding, and took her to the hospital, where she spent ten weeks in bed. Had the phone not been in her pocket, she may have bled to death, as no one else was home and wouldn't be for hours. I do believe the fragrance of funeral home flowers I smelled simultaneously was a warning to pray against death.

There is no Scripture that says angels bring a special fragrance. However, any type of sweet fragrance that is not normal or from a known source could be a "sign" of some kind, as there are "signs, wonders, and miracles" (Heb. 2:4) and something of this nature would be a "wonder."

15. Are angels generational, in the sense that they remain with one family for generations?

I will answer this from two opposing sides. In the spirit world, there is a type of spirit known as a "familiar spirit," mentioned sixteen times in the Old Testament. They operate through witches and sorcerers as indicated in 1 Samuel 28, when the witch of Endor attempted to contact the dead through a familiar spirit. They can be familiar with people, places, and situations and connected with an unconverted family for generations. This could be a clue as to why certain sins continue in a family for generations, as these spirits create strongholds of bondage.

Concerning angels, when Jacob was blessing Ephraim and Manasseh, he prayed: "The Angel which redeemed me from all evil, bless the lads; and let my name be named on them, and the name of my fathers Abraham and Isaac; and let them grow into a multitude in the midst of the earth" (Gen. 48:16).

Jacob requested that the angel who was with him continue to bless and be with the next generation. There was a special angel with Abraham, too, and we see steady angelic activity in the life of Jacob. There is no reason to believe that these were two different angels, but instead an angel assigned to the early patriarchs who gave instruction, warnings, and direction to ensure that the will of God would be completed.

God thinks generationally. When He gave Abraham the promise of a future nation, He said the blessing would be passed to Abraham's "seed," which refers to his descendants (Gen.12:7, 13:15, 15:18). He promises blessings to you, your children, and their children's children (Ezek. 37:25; Acts 2:39). It is possible a generational angel can be assigned to a godly family.

16. Why do people seem to encounter demonic spirits more than angels?

This question is interesting and does appear to be true. Before they became believers, many Christians describe seeing some form of dark spirits, either as dark shadows in the form of a man, or a manifestation of an evil spirit, yet few believers have actually seen an angel of the Lord.

The first reason that comes to mind is that angels carry not only the presence of God, but the *holiness* of God. There are living creatures and seraphim angels continually standing before God's throne crying, "Holy, holy, holy, is the Lord" (Isa. 6:1–4). Holiness denotes being separated and set apart, meaning God is superior, and set apart from all other "gods." Old Testament holiness required a cutting apart from what was unclean, either in character or in ritual form. Certain foods and actions were unclean. God's holiness denotes His moral and spiritual perfection and His willingness to judge righteously mankind's imperfections.

When angels appeared to Moses in the burning bush in the Median desert and to Joshua near Gilgal in Jericho, they demanded that these men remove their shoes, as the ground they were on was "holy." There was nothing "holy" about the actual ground, other than the angels being present on it. Thus the angels made the ground holy.

Demons, on the other hand, are unclean, and attracted to sin or our sin nature. Because the works, character, and nature of mankind lean toward disobedience and sin, there are more open doors and portals for demon spirits to enter. Although these spirits are invisible, the veil on the eyes of individuals must be lifted to see into the spirit world. Certain drugs seem to open a portal in the brain that enables people to see the invisible world. At times, the Lord allows us to see demonic powers to acknowledge the actual spirit behind the struggle. Both totally unconverted individuals and backsliders have seen demon entities, and when they did, great fear overcame them. They turned to God and understood the reality of the spirit world and what they were battling.

Angels are more apt to manifest when a person is dedicating themselves to God's service through fasting and prayer, or when the presence of the Holy Spirit is strong and individuals are in a condition of humility and repentance, which is the doorway to holiness or the separation of the base elements of this world.

17. Why does it seem people from other nations tend to experience more of the supernatural?

The world is divided between Western and Eastern thought. In the West, in our academic institutions of "higher learning," liberal professors often begin instilling unbelief and doubt in the minds of their students toward the supernatural, especially Biblical narratives. This is also true in many schools teaching theology. Some of the highest levels of unbelief come from those with the highest education. Thus in the West, the heart and mind are closed in unbelief, where God does not manifest His presence. In Nazareth, Jesus could do not mighty miracles because of their unbelief. Zacharias was smote with the inability to speak because of his unbelief toward the message of an angel (Luke 1). Spiritual unbelief is the highest level of insult toward God.

People from the nations in the East tend to have a stronger

belief in the supernatural, including the world of angels and demons. Some major Eastern religions use charms and incantations to drive away evil spirits and have strong beliefs in heaven, hell, demons, and angels. While many of their beliefs are corrupt and inaccurate from a Biblical perspective, they are "open" in their minds and hearts toward the supernatural realm. Thus it becomes easier for both evil spirits and angelic spirits to manifest.

For example, there are hundreds of stories that can be told of how Muslims experienced dreams and visions of Christ, and in some instances an angel appeared and pointed the person to Christ as the only true Messiah of the world. One of my personal friends, a former devout Muslim for fifty years, was dying in a hospital when one evening a man came into his room and carried on a conversation with him, explaining every question he had concerning Christ. He converted and later found out there was no doctor in his room. He says the person was Christ, and had appeared in the same manner he had to Saul on the road to Damascus. I believe when a person is more open to believing in the spirit realm, it is easier for them to be receptive to manifestations, whether they are good or bad.

18. How fast can an angel of protection move during a situation, such as a sudden car accident?

There are several aspects of this answer. The first question would be, if an angel intervenes, was it a generational angel assigned to a godly family, or one in the area when the accident occurred, or one assigned to prevent a premature death? This would be difficult to answer, and only God would know the specific messenger sent to assist in protecting the family or individual.

The second question would concern how much foreknowledge there was and how much preparation was made to assist in protecting the person(s). Was the will of God for them being preserved in saving their life? Or was the accident so sudden that an angel was required in a flash of time? Because God knows all things, I am certain He is aware of any accident prior to it occurring, as nothing can take Him by surprise.

The third aspect is how swiftly an angel can arrive to a scene. Angels can move as fast as lightning (Ezek. 1), which is over 186,000 miles per second. The earth is about 25,000 miles in circumference at the equator, so at the speed of light, one angel could circle the equator about seven times in one second. This is how it is possible for the Lord to send you an angel within a few seconds when you cry out to Him for help in a sudden and dangerous situation.

When Gabriel was sent to Daniel, he came from the third heaven, which is millions of light-years away, and he was in the atmosphere of Babylon within one day. This type of travel would require either some type of unknown opening in the universe (a heavenly portal) or travel at the speed of thought, which cannot be measured outside of earth's time dimension.

19. If we have asked God to send angels to protect our children, how do we know they are doing it?

This is where faith and trust play a role. There are numerous promises in Scripture that say if we ask anything according to God's will, He hears us (1 John 5:14). The will of God is seen in the verse "The angel of the Lord encamps around about those that fear the Lord and delivers them" (Ps. 34:7). Christ taught that if we ask the Father anything in His name, He will do it (John 14:14), and when we ask, we must believe it before we receive it (Mark 11:24). We cannot ask in faith and the next day speak unbelief. In my life, I know God has heard me when I can rest in peace and leave things in His hands.

However, I never ignore a burden of danger when I sense it. I will break away from my routine to pray in advance. Recently, I was burdened for six days with knowing someone was going to pass away in a certain family, despite no member being sick, and no other evidence the death could or would occur. I told the family that it would occur while they were in Israel on a tour. Near the conclusion of their trip, they received a phone call from a family member saying that a relative had been killed in an accident. I did not have any inclination to pray for an angel, but I believe the Lord allowed me to sense this to prepare them for what occurred.

At times, when praying, divine intervention occurs. When we ask God for angelic protection over our loved ones, we must believe He has heard us and believe the Covenant promise. When Jesus and his disciples were on a boat in the middle of a lake and He said, "Let us go over to the other side," a storm hit and the boat filled with water; yet Jesus was asleep in the hull. The disciples were fearful because they forgot the promise that said the "other side." Jesus was not afraid because he knew the storm would not sink the boat—so he slept. Confidence in God's promises will cause us to enter into a "rest" in our spirit.

20. I often asked the Lord to protect my family but a child was killed. Did God let me down and why?

Many godly men and women have experienced the death of a child. Oral Roberts lost his oldest son in a tragedy. Oral's daughter and son-in-law were killed in a plane crash, and his son Richard lost a child shortly after it was born. Yet Oral had tremendous results in praying for and seeing miracles.

Elisha received a "double portion" of Elijah's anointing, and at death, his bones raised a dead soldier. Yet, the Bible says, he died of a sickness. If his bones raised the dead, why couldn't the anointing heal him? My father, Fred Stone, prayed and saw sixteen people healed from cancer by God's power, yet his body shut down from diabetes. Dad told me, "My body at age seventy-seven may be shutting down, but tell everyone God is still a healer!"

There are many answers as to "why" something bad occurs. Years ago, on a Saturday morning, I headed out the door to take my car down some mountain roads to pray and just clear my mind. As I headed out, I heard the Holy Spirit say, "Not today. You will be in an accident if you go!" I knew His voice, so I turned around and walked back into the house. A few weeks later I did the same thing—headed out the door and heard the voice say, "Not today. You will be in an accident." I tried to ignore it and my spirit became heavy. I stopped and had a vision that lasted about two seconds where I saw a bridge I cross on my mountain rides. A big truck lost control, crossed the line, and hit me head on. My heart began pounding and I didn't leave the house. A few weeks later, I headed out the door with no burden and drove the road with no problems. Often, good people ignore "warning signals" or those deep-felt burdens, and override them to their own demise. Any strong burden in your spirit is a sign of some danger or problem on the horizon.

At times, people go against their better judgment. One of my pastor friends as a young man was about to board a small plane in Kentucky with his best friend, his brother, and his father who pastored a huge church in Ohio, where they were headed. A storm was passing and the owners of the airport told the dad to let the storm pass first, but he replied, "I can't miss church in the morning." My friend followed the advice not to fly and instead drove back to Ohio with other friends. The small plane never made it back, as it crashed in the storm and the pastor and his two sons were killed. If we ignore senses of danger and go ahead with our plans, we cannot blame God if something goes wrong.

When Paul boarded a ship headed to Rome, he warned the captain they shouldn't go because there were winter storms on the Mediterranean and the journey would be dangerous. The captain ignored Paul, and in the middle of their trip a massive typhoon hit, and without angelic intervention, Paul and the entire ship with over 200 on board would have sunk in the sea!

It is possible for a good person to be in the wrong place at the wrong time, or for a prayer burden to be ignored. In the busyness of life, we can miss the voice of God helping us prevent future trouble. I have been warned a few times in dreams of spiritual conflicts coming but in my early ministry did not pay attention to the warning and suffered for a season from my ignorance.

In the early church, James died and Peter was spared. God did not love Peter more than James. However, the church heard of the death threat, prayed nonstop, and experienced a spiritual breakthrough on Peter's behalf.

Paul escaped danger on numerous occasions, described in Acts, including being lowered in a basket over a wall in Damascus, escaping at night on horseback from a death threat, and surviving a shipwreck and a poisonous snakebite, yet he was beheaded in Rome and not rescued from the jail as Peter was. At first, Paul said he knew God was able to deliver him, and in his final epistle written to Timothy, he said he was "now ready to be offered," meaning he was accepting his martyrdom.

In Hebrews 11, Paul lists the faith heroes of the Bible. He speaks of the miraculous feats and answers to prayer they experienced. He then speaks of others who were not rescued and were tortured and died. He said they did not accept deliverance but desired a "better resurrection," which alludes to a martyr's crown, the highest level of sacrifice.

There could be various reasons why bad things happen, and there is not one simple explanation. However, when a friend of mine lost a beautiful daughter in a plane crash, a fellow minister who experienced that same tragedy called him. He was told not to begin questioning why, as he would ask that the rest of his life. He was told that only the Lord knew things about the accident that no one else understood and those questions would be answered one day in eternity.

21. In Revelation, there are three angels, including one who preaches the gospel. Why does this angel preach, when preaching of the gospel was only assigned to men?

Revelation 14:6 says, "And I saw another angel fly in the midst of heaven, having the everlasting gospel to preach unto them that dwell on the earth, and to every nation, and kindred, and tongue, and people." The first of the three angels in John's vision comes down preaching the "everlasting gospel." The second announces the fall of Babylon (14:8) and the third warns men not to take the mark of the beast because, if they do, they will be eternally doomed (14:9–10). Prior to this narrative, we read where two men called the "two witnesses" are testifying in Jerusalem for forty-two months, pronouncing judgments and wrath upon any men who seek to harm them. After that time, they are slain by the Antichrist (Rev. 11:3–7). The question becomes if the church is the earthly agent to preach the gospel, then why are we not preaching it in Revelation 14, and instead the angels are bringing the messages to all men?

The Greek word for "angel" (*aggelos*) is also translated as a "human messenger," as is the case when John the Baptist is called "my messenger" (Matt. 1:10; Mark 1:2; Luke 2:7). Some people who hold a post-tribulation view suggest the angels in Revelation are human ministers, and are not heavenly beings. One phrase in the text hinders that possible interpretation when it reads, "I saw an angel flying in the midst of heaven . . ." This messenger is not on earth, but in heaven declaring the message. Since men on earth hear and see these angels, they may appear in the form of men, but are nonetheless heavenly beings.

Angels might be needed to preach when the church and all "overcomers" have been taken to heaven in the great catching away (1 Thess. 4:16–17), and the two prophets that ministered for forty-two months have been slain and caught up to heaven (Rev. 11), leaving no earthly minister to preach the gospel and warn humans. God will commission three special angels to perform the task of presenting the gospel and give people the final warning not to worship the beast or receive his mark. Angels were present at creation and will continue in their ministry into eternity. The Bible speaks of the final doom of Satan, his angels, and unrepentant men. The third angel warns of the lake of fire, and says if people worship the beast, they shall be "tormented with fire and brimstone in the presence of the holy angels and the presence of the lamb" (Rev. 14:9–10). The ministry and the presence of holy angels will never cease.

Scholars note in Revelation 12 that Satan has charge over one-third of the angels, a group that was expelled from heaven along with Satan in ages past (Rev. 12:1–4). These angels are considered "fallen" (Jude 6; 2 Pet. 2:4). With one-third aligned with Satan, two-thirds remain that have stayed faithful to the

Almighty God and assist him in various assignments in heaven and on earth. Whether these be cherubim (Ezek. 10), seraphim (Isa. 6:1–4), ministering spirits (Heb. 1:14), or another form of angelic being, we have two angels for us for every angel who followed Satan in the downfall, meaning there will always be more with us than against us (2 Kings 6:16).

Angels were present at the time of the earth's creation (Job 38:4–7) and will continue their ministry assignments and special activities during the future Great Tribulation, when many of the final end-time prophecies will be fulfilled. The world has entered a new season of prophetic movement coupled with the fulfillment of many ancient prophecies, indication that this is the season of angels.

CONCLUSION

I wish to conclude this book with the following practical insights based on the Bible:

1. Angels are real and are assigned for ministry. We often do not ask God for their assistance, but we should when we sense a particular need.

2. If Satan took one-third of the angels under his control during his rebellion, there are two-thirds that remained loyal to God. This fact indicates that for every evil agent in the kingdom of darkness, there are two angels who are *for* us. Thus, there are always more for us than against us (2 Kings).

3. The ministry of angels will increase during the prophetic seasons we are entering. It is clear that the powers of darkness will increase their intensity of war against the saints, as Satan knows he is running out of time (Rev. 12). We are told that where sin abounds, grace does more abound (Rom. 5:20), and when the enemy comes in like a flood, the Spirit of the Lord will lift up a standard against him (Isa. 59:19). As the battle increases against dark forces, God will send his angels to engage in warfare.

ABOUT THE AUTHOR

Perry Stone is the bestselling author of numerous books, including *The Code of the Holy Spirit* and *How to Interpret Dreams and Visions*. He directs one of America's fastest-growing ministries, the Voice of Evangelism. An international evangelist, Perry holds a BA in theology from Covenant Life Christian College. He lives in Cleveland, Tennessee, with his wife, Pam.